Invertebrates of
Dokdo Island
Mollusks

Sa Heung Kim

He received his Ph.D. from the Department of Biological Sciences at Seoul National University. He is also the research director of In The Sea Inc and the adjunct professor at the Dept. of Biology, Gyeongsang National University.

Yong Tae Kim

He graduated from the Dept. of Education at Korea University and is the director of the technology development team of In The Sea Inc.

Hack Cheul Kim

He graduated from the Dept. of Physical Education at Kyunghee University. Currently, he is the director of the operation team of In The Sea Inc.

Jongrak Lee

He completed his Ph.D. in Biology at Sungkyunkwan University. Currently, he is the director of the general support team of In The Sea Inc.

Date of Issue October 2020

Author Sa Heung Kim, Yong Tae Kim, Hack Cheul Kim, Jongrak Lee

Photographer Sa Heung Kim, Yong Tae Kim, Hack Cheul Kim, Jongrak Lee

Project Staff Tae Seo Park, Sang-Hoon Han, Jin-Han Kim

Publishing Organization Gyeongsangbuk-do Provincial Government

Research Institute National Institute of Biological Science (conducted by In The Sea Inc.)

Address of Publishing Organization 90, Yongheung-ro, Buk-gu, Pohang City, Gyeongsangbuk-do Province, Republic of Korea

Tel: (82) 054-880-7753 / Fax: (82) 054-246-9058

Translation Institute of Translation and Interpretation of Handong Global University

Printing Youngshinsa

ISBN 979-11-951334-9-9 (93470)

Invertebrates of Dokdo Island

Dokdo Island

Mollusks

Sa Heung Kim

Yong Tae Kim

Hack Cheul Kim

Jongrak Lee

GYEONGSANGBUK-DO

Foreword

Dokdo, a towering island in the middle of the East Sea of Korea, is the first place in the Republic of Korea to see the sunrise each day. It consists of two main islands, Dongdo (East Island) and Seodo (West Island), and 89 annexed islands.

Formed by underwater volcanic eruptions, Dokdo has never been connected to the mainland; as such, it has a unique natural environment. Its coast is where the cold-water currents from North Korea meet the warm water from the East Sea, which makes it home to a variety of marine life. To preserve this valuable natural environment and its various ecosystems, the Ministry of Environment has designated Dokdo as Special Island No.1.

Dokdo's biological resources have great potential value due to their uniqueness. However, it is often difficult to survey Dokdo's biodiversity in a systematic manner because the number of days each year during which biodiversity surveys can be conducted is limited due to the inclement weather conditions. For this reason, the biota of Dokdo has not yet been fully explored, and a lot of it remains uncharted territory.

Despite this, the National Institute of Biological Resources (NIBR) has been conducting research to systematically identify the species inhabiting Dokdo and surrounding areas since 2013. As a result, NIBR has published three books in the *Invertebrates of Dokdo Island* series: *104 Species of Mollusca from Dokdo Island* in 2014, *143 Species of Macro-Crustaceans from Dokdo Island* in 2017, and *23 Species of Cnidaria and 29 Species of Echinodermata from Dokdo Island* in 2018.

Gyeongsangbuk-do Province, with the permission of NIBR, has decided to publish an English version of *Invertebrates of Dokdo Island*. This book, the first of the series, introduces 104 species of Mollusca from Dokdo Island, each accompanied by photographs. This book will allow readers to gain new knowledge about both mollusks and the uniqueness of Dokdo's marine ecosystem. We at Gyeongsandbuk-do Province will spare no effort in sharing information about the status of the biological resources in Dokdo and its precious value.

I would like to express my gratitude to NIBR for understanding the need to publish this book in English and for providing their full support and to the researchers for putting in a great deal of effort even in the face of numerous limitations and difficulties. I hope this illustrated book will be widely used to help readers all over the world to better understand the wildlife on Dokdo because many have devoted themselves to making this book a reality. Thank you.

October 2020

Lee Cheol-woo, Governor of Gyeongsangbuk-do

Preface

I remember the first time I went into the ocean. Under the water, it was hard to breathe or move, but the dark blue frame in front of me was clearly engraved in my mind. The sea, which has long been wrapped in a thick fog, has started to reveal itself only now. This book is based on my twenty-year experience. I had been meaning to write it for quite some time, and I finally made it happen.

The structure of *Invertebrates of Dokdo Island* differs from previous publications. First of all, the uniqueness of Dokdo is prioritized in this book. Many of the marine invertebrates found on Dokdo have been reported before, but often they have been grouped with those of Ulleungdo or only representative species of certain taxa have been described. Thus, an overview of the invertebrate biodiversity on Dokdo specifically was desperately needed.

Secondly, a significant taxon needed to be selected, and we chose Mollusca without hesitation. Describing this phylum can be more complicated than it appears. Compared to other taxa, it is not especially difficult to access information at a general level; they are easy to find and a large volume of data is available for identification. However, morphological similarities between related species or variants within the same species can be easily overlooked, which can result in errors in species identification. For these reasons, previous lists of Dokdo mollusk species published thus far have been unreliable.

Thirdly, there was also the photography issue. Images are an important component that can determine the success or failure of a book like this one. We decided to take photographs of every single species in the book. We have been in and out of the waters for over twenty years, and it was a matter of pride for our team. We never even thought twice about it.

With that final decision, we (perhaps foolishly) chose the most difficult path for an illustrated guide. This book is probably the first that solely focuses on mollusks ever published in South Korea. We took photographs from gastropods the size of rice grains to cephalopods the size of the human body until we were satisfied. This was not something only we could achieve, but it was definitely something that would be more difficult for others to do.

While finalizing the text, I still saw some room for improvement. The new experiences and knowledge I gained in the process of writing the book made some of it seem like wastepaper, and this sense of frustration grew stronger as the deadline approached. "Ah! I have just learned something new again." Writing this book, I sighed like I would never sigh again. A small comfort is that I tried my best to get everything right.

I express my gratitude to the National Institute of Biological Resources for planning the publication, to Gyeongsangbuk-do Provincial Government for publishing the English version and to GeoBook for willingly taking on the production. I also thank my long-time friend Jeong Bong-kwon, who took care of our long journey to Dokdo as the owner of Ulleung Diver Resort. Most of all, my biggest thanks go to my colleagues, who were generous enough to let me write this preface even though they worked harder than I did.

Looking back, we have been everywhere, whether it be in or out of the water. Yet, we will not stop here. Building on this book, which is really just the first step, we plan to introduce the groups of marine invertebrates that we have found underwater one by one. If I were to choose the most important thing that I have learned throughout my journey here, it would be the identification of species. This is a philosophy, and perhaps the alpha and omega of biodiversity.

Kim Sa Heung, Lead Author

Contents

005 Foreword

006 Preface

010 Mollusks of Dokdo

015 Glossary

024 Class Polyplacophora

026 Ischnochiton (Haploplax) comptus

028 Ischnochiton (Ischnochiton) boninensis

030 Lepidozona coreanica

032 Placiphorella stimpsoni

034 Mopalia retifera

036 Chiton (Rhyssoplax) kurodai

038 Liolophura japonica

040 Onithochiton hirasei

042 Acanthochitona circellata

044 Cryptoplax japania

046 Class Gastropoda

048 Haliotis discus

050 Haliotis supertexta

052 Tugali decussata

054 Macroschisma dilatatum

056 Chlorostoma lischkei

058 Chlorostoma turbinatum

060 Tegula pfeifferi

062 Omphalius rusticus

064 Cantharidus bisbalteatus

066 Cantharidus jessoensis

068 Cantharidus japonicus

070 Monodonta perplexa

072 Stomatolina rubra

074 Calliostoma multiliratum

076 Calliostoma unicum

078 Homalopoma amussitatum

080 Granata lyrate

082 Turbo cornutus

084 Pomaulax japonicus

086 Cellana grata

088 Cellana toreuma

090 Lottia dorsuosa

092 Nipponacmea schrenckii

094 Niveotectura pallida

096 Crepidula onyx

098 Purpuradusta gracilis

100 Littorina brevicula

102 Echinolittorina radiata

104 Hipponix conicus

106 Sandalia triticea

108 Thylacodes adamsii

110 Monoplex parthenopeus

112 Reishia bronni

114 Reishia clavigera

116 Reishia luteostoma

118 Ceratostoma roriflum

120 Ergalatax contracta

122 Mitrella bicincta

124 Nassarius fraterculus

126 Engina menkeana

128 Kelletia lischkei

130 Pollia subrubiginosa

132 Haminoea japonica

134 Elysia atroviridis

136 Elysia abei

138 Aplysia kurodai

140 Aplysia juliana

142 Aplysia parvula

144 Pleurobranchaea japonica

146 Berthellina citrina

148   *Okenia hiroi*

150   *Platydoris ellioti*

152   *Cadlina japonica*

154   *Homoiodoris japonica*

156   *Chromodoris orientalis*

158   *Goniobranchus tinctorius*

160   *Goniobranchus aureopurpureus*

162   *Hypselodoris festiva*

164   *Aldisa cooperi*

166   *Dendrodoris krusensternii*

168   *Dermatobranchus otome*

170   *Tritonia festiva*

172   *Hermissenda crassicornis*

174   *Sakuraeolis japonica*

176   *Protaeolidiella atra*

178   *Siphonaria sirius*

180   *Siphonaria japonica*

182   **Class Bivalvia**

184   *Arca boucardi*

186   *Porterius dalli*

188   *Mytilus coruscus*

190   *Leiosolennus lischkei*

192   *Modiolus modiolus*

194   *Modiolus nipponicus*

196   *Septifer keenae*

198   *Septifer virgatus*

200   *Laevichlamys cuneata*

202   *Spondylus squamosus*

204   *Limaria hirasei*

206   *Neopycnodonte cochlear*

208   *Striostrea cicumpicta*

210   *Crassostrea gigas*

212   *Crassostrea nippona*

214   *Anomia chinensis*

216   *Chama japonica*

218   *Kellia porculus*

220   *Cardita leana*

222   *Solen gordonis*

224   *Gari kazusensis*

226   *Irus irus*

228   *Paphia vernicosa*

230   *Gorbula venusta*

232   *Hiatella arctica*

234   *Entodesma navicular*

236   **Class Cephalopoda**

238   *Octopus vulgaris*

240   List of Dokdo's mollusks

250   Literature

252   Scientific names

Gajebawi Rock of Dokdo (depth 22m)

Mollusks of Dokdo

Dokdo is a small remote island of South Korea, located about 216.8 km from the nearest mainland county in Korea (Uljin in Gyeongbuk Province) and 87.4 km from Ulleungdo. Dokdo is volcanic in origin, produced by volcanic activity in the East Sea. Marine organisms have adapted to this environment for over 2 million years. The marine invertebrates of Dokdo consist of 50% temperate species, 23% widely-distributed species, 20% southern (i.e., tropical) species, and 7% northern species. Therefore, Dokdo seems to be more affected by warm currents despite its location on the outskirts of the East Sea. Of the southern species, which can be used as indicators of the effects of warm currents, the order Decapoda account for 50% and mollusks for 7%. Most mollusks are temperate or widely distributed (i.e., cosmopolitan).

Geographical distribution type

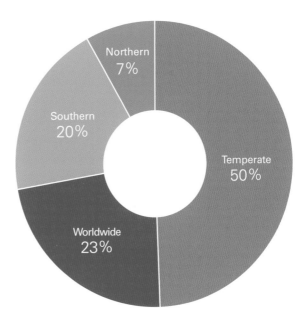

Since the first two species of decapods – *Pachygrapsus crassipes* and *Pagusus similis* (now *P. rubrior*) – were reported by Kim Hoon-Soo (1960), about 405 species of invertebrates in Dokdo, including those surveyed by Kyungpook National University, have been reported (Ryu et al., 2012). Mollusks, which are covered in this book, are a phylum that is very familiar to mankind and is commonly used as a source of food. More than 100,000 species are known worldwide, with a further 35,000 species believed to have gone extinct. Approximately 1,500 species have been recorded in Korea.

In terms of mollusks on Dokdo, Kim (1978) reported a total of seven species, two polyplacophorans and five gastropods, for the first time. Based on many subsequent studies (Kim and Choe, 1981; Son and Hong, 1992; Choe and Lee, 1994; Choe et al., 1996; Lee and Seo, 2006; Hwang, 2007), 135 species had been identified on Dokdo before this book was begun. Subsequently, the list of mollusk species on Dokdo was revised in the process of producing this book, and a total of 173 species have been identified. Of these, those species that need to be reviewed, including those whose scientific name has changed or those with an undefined habitat, are highlighted in a list at the back of this book.

The most representative mollusk species in Dokdo are summarized here. Mussels (*Mytilus corsucus*) form the largest colonies at a depth of 5–15 m, while oysters (*Crassostrea nippona* or *Striostrea circumpicta*) form communities at around 20 m. *Arca boucardi* also forms colonies at this depth. At 25 m, *Neopycnodonte cochlear* dominates, though these colonies are smaller than those on Ulleungdo. These adherent species are of great ecological value in that they provide habitat for other marine invertebrates and fish.

Dokdo is home to various types of sea hares and slugs (Order Nudibranchia). *Sakuraeolis japonica* mainly feeds on *Solanderia misakiensis*, while *Hermissenda crassicornis* is commonly found in colonies of *Fukaurahydra anthoformis*. Of the migratory species, the turban shell (*Turbo cornutus*) is the most prominent, and *Aplysia parvula* and *Aplysia* spp. are also commonly encountered. Dokdo is a stable habitat for various marine invertebrates, particularly those based around colonies of large adherent mollusks.

This book describes 104 species of mollusk, including 10 species from the class Polyplacophora, 67 from Gastropoda, 26 from Bivalvia, and 1 from Cephalopoda. The names given in Korean characters in this book represent the commonly used name in Korea, while the traits and behaviour of the species are explained using more easily understandable Korean words rather than Sino-Korean characters. Species names and other taxonomic classifications are based on information from the World Register of Marine Species (WoRMS). New names were given for taxa without Korean names and, if there were no representative taxa within a subcategory, the Korean name is not indicated. The characteristics and behaviour of invertebrates, including mollusks, are often difficult to describe. As a solution to this, photos are used, with the distinguishing traits indicated. To establish the Korean and global distribution of the species, books by Choe (1992), EOL (2014), Habe (1977), Min (2004), Okutani (2000), and Rudman (2000) were consulted, including the confirmed cases by the authors of this book. We also reviewed the list of 163 mollusk species from Dokdo, and found 41 cases where the scientific name had changed, 1 case where there was no scientific names, 1 case of misidentification, and 27 cases of an undetermined habitat. With the 10 newly confirmed species found while taking photographs for this book, 173 species were finally listed.

Symbol

EN Endangered species

RA Rare species

ES Endemic species

IV Invasive species

🍴 Edible

T Temperate

W Worldwide

S Southern

N Northern

Population
(5: very high; 4: high; 3: moderate; 2: low; 1: rare)
*Population is based on Dokdo

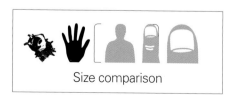

Size comparison

Glossary

Gastropoda

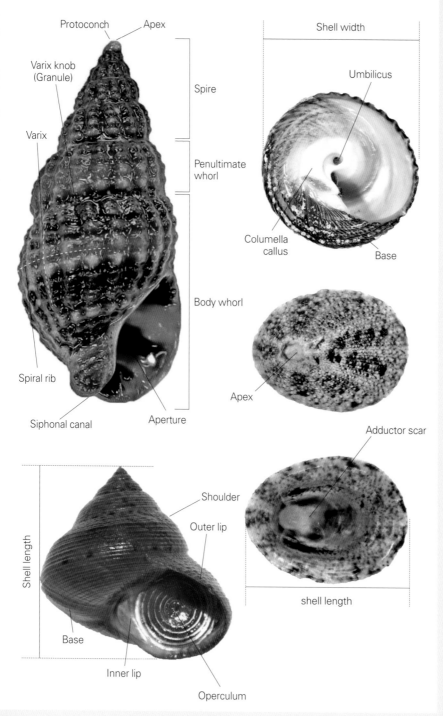

Protoconch
Apex
Varix knob (Granule)
Spire
Varix
Penultimate whorl
Body whorl
Spiral rib
Siphonal canal
Aperture

Shell width
Umbilicus
Columella callus
Base

Apex

Adductor scar
shell length

Shoulder
Outer lip
Shell length
Base
Inner lip
Operculum

Gastropoda

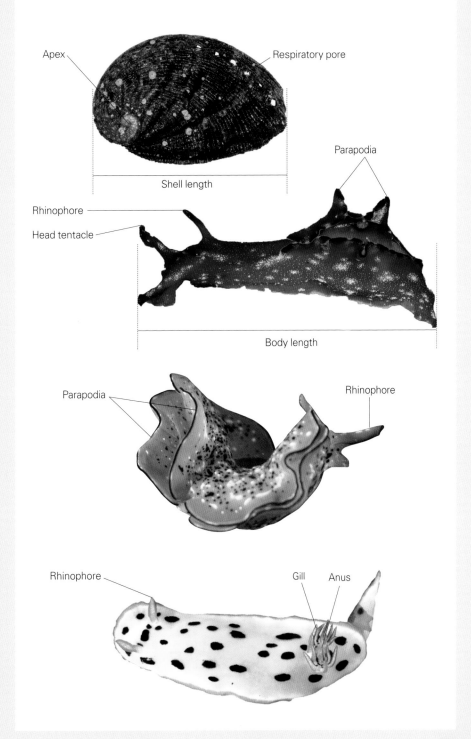

Apex

Respiratory pore

Shell length

Parapodia

Rhinophore

Head tentacle

Body length

Parapodia

Rhinophore

Rhinophore

Gill   Anus

Bivalvia

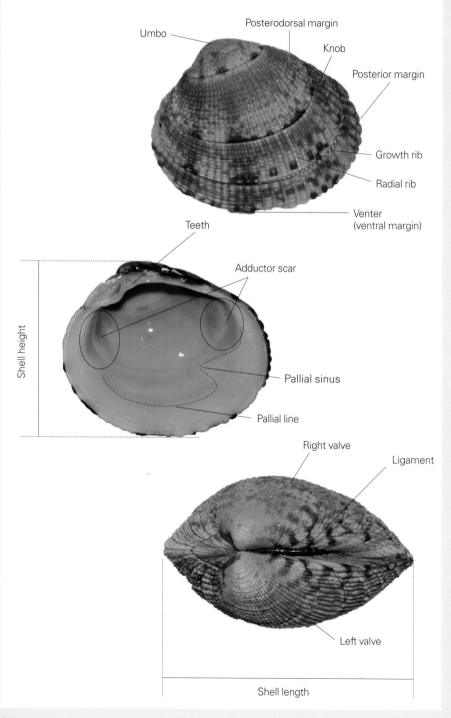

Umbo

Posterodorsal margin

Knob

Posterior margin

Growth rib

Radial rib

Venter
(ventral margin)

Teeth

Adductor scar

Shell height

Pallial sinus

Pallial line

Right valve

Ligament

Left valve

Shell length

Bivalvia

Auricle Umbo

Left valve

Shell length

Resilium

Deeply
notched

Right valve

Shell height

Umbo

Resilium

Adductor scar

Shell length

Polyplacophora

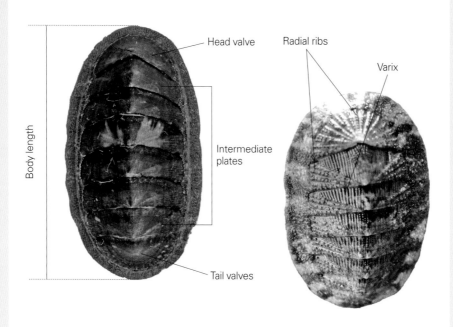

Head valve

Radial ribs

Varix

Body length

Intermediate plates

Tail valves

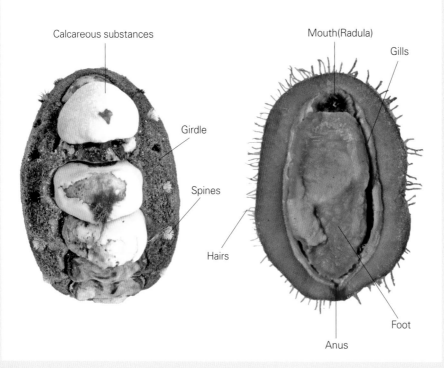

Calcareous substances

Mouth(Radula)

Gills

Girdle

Spines

Hairs

Anus

Foot

Adductor scar
The mark on the interior of the shell where the muscle that closes the bivalve shell is attached. The adductor muscles at the front and back are called the anterior adductor muscle and the posterior adductor muscle, respectively.

Aperture
The main opening in the gastropod shell where the head and foot emerges. The margin of the aperture is called the lip, which consists of an outer and inner lip.

Apex/Umbo
The extremity of a shell, representing its oldest part. The apex of the gastropod shell is at the top in a standing position; in Bivalvia, it is the beginning of the concentric circle, which is called the umbo.

Base
The lower margin of the gastropod shell. It usually refers to the shell bottom when it stands upright.

Columella callus
The enamel-secreting smooth whorl on the inner lip of a gastropod.

Dorsal margin
The edge on the dorsal side from the umbo of Bivalvia. The back of the umbo is called the posterodorsal margin; the posterior end from which the atrial siphon emerges is called the posterior margin; the lower edge of the shell is called the ventral margin.

Girdle
The rigid fleshy rim surrounding the shell plates on the dorsum of a chiton. Well-developed scales are present in the girdle.

Growth rib
A growth ring on the shell surface produced due to differences in the growth rate of the shell. It grows across the shell. Depending on the depth of the ridge, it can be classified as a growth line, growth cord, or growth rib.

Head shield
The flat shield in front of the head of chitons used to dig into sand or other substrates.

Head tentacle
The sensory organ on the head of a sea slug. The tentacles that develop above the head are called rhinophores.

Head valve
The first of the eight shell plates of a chiton. The last plate is called the tail plate.

Knob
A rounded tubercle that forms on the shell surface when the spiral rib and varix cross (the radial and growth ribs in Bivalvia). Small knobs are called granules.

Ligament
The leathery protrusions on the dorsal edge. The ligament opens the shells of Bivalvia, while the adductor muscle closes them.

Ligamental ridge
The raised part of the lower umbo in the interior of the shell.

Operculum
The organ of a sea snail that protects the molluscan (soft) body by blocking the aperture.

Pallial line
Traces of the mantle muscle attached to the shell. The mantle refers to the membrane surrounding the visceral mass attached to the bivalve shell.

Pallial sinus
The vestige of the mantle in the interior of a bivalve shell. The indentation differs between species.

Parapodia
The wings on the side of the body of a sea hare or sea slug.

Periphery
The perimeter of the body whorl, which is the widest.

Protoconch
The first one or two whorls around the apex, representing the oldest part of the shell. Adults may often have an eroded protoconch.

Radial rib
The thick ridge radially extending from the umbo of Bivalvia.

Radula
Except for Bivalvia, the organ for feeding unique to mollusks. It is a structure combining teeth and a tongue.

Resilium
The triangular leathery ligament located below the umbo in the interior of the shell of scallops. It is also called the inner ligament. The depression bearing the resilium is called the resilium in chondrophores.

Respiratory pore
The respiratory opening found in abalones and keyhole limpets.

Right valve
The shell on the right side when holding the shell so that the side with the ligament (where the siphonal canal is) faces up. The left shell is called the left valve.

Shell length
The length from the apex to the aperture. The shell length of Bivalvia is measured from the front end to the rear end; its shell height is the length from the ventral side to the dorsal side.

Shell plate
A shell composed of eight plates, which are well developed in chitons. The first plate is called the head valve, the last plate is the tail valve, and the middle ones are the intermediate valves.

Shoulder
The angulate corner on the spiral whorl of gastropods.

Siphonal canal
The groove or tube-like organ in front of the aperture of gastropods that takes in water. Usually, it protrudes in front of the aperture.

Spiral rib
A spirally (horizontally) developed ridge on the spiral whorl. A thin rib is called a spiral riblet; a rib forming a valley is called a spiral groove. The spiral line is thinner than the spiral riblet.

Spiral whorl
The whorls on a gastropod shell. The first and largest whorl is called the body whorl, and the next whorl is called the penultimate whorl. The portion from the body whorl to the apex is called the spire.

Suture
The border between the spiral whorls of gastropods.

Teeth
The primary and lateral structures in bivalves that prevent the shells from twisting or intertwining.

Umbilicus
The navel-shaped hole or trace at the center of a gastropod. While the protoconch continually grows into whorls, the umbilicus forms at the center of the interior of the body whorl.

Varix
A longitudinal ridge on the apex or whorls of a gastropod. If it is horizontal, it is called a spiral rib; in a bivalve, the varix is a radial rib and the spiral rib is the growth rib.

Class Polyplacophora

The name Polyplacophora derives from the words "poly" (many), "placo" (plate), and "phora" (bearing). The species in this class, which are collectively referred to as chitons, have eight (rarely seven) flat shell plates made of calcium carbonate that cover the dorsum like tiled roof. The head has degenerated, eyes and tentacles are absent, and a radula is present in the mouth. The inside of the foot is large and flat, looking like an oval sucker.

More than 900 species are known worldwide, and 20 species from five families have been reported in Korea. The species in Korea are usually less than 7-8 cm in length, with the largest chiton (*Cryptochiton stelleri*) in the world being about 30 cm. It lives from the intertidal zone to a depth of 4,000 m, while Korean species are mainly found in shallow waters.

Ischnochiton (*Haploplax*) *comptus* (Gould, 1859)

5 m depth

EN
RA
ES
IV
S

Morphology

Body small to medium, elongate-oval. Shell plates large, girdle narrow, with fine radial lines on surface. Color dark chestnut to brown. Head valve bearing 50-60 radial wrinkles, crossing faint concentric growth lines. BL: about 25 mm

Remarks

Called the chiton or loricates in some local areas, it has eight dorsal shell plates, unlike sea snails or bivalves. It is mainly found under rocks from the middle or lower intertidal zone to the shallow subtidal zone. In general, individuals of this species found on Dokdo are smaller in size than those living in the West or South Sea of Korea.

Distribution

This species is found in tropical and subtropical regions, including Korea, Japan (south Hokkaido to Okinawa), China, Taiwan, the Philippines, Indonesia, Australia, southern India, and the west coast of central Africa. Given its geographical distribution, it is a southern species, and is commonly observed in Korea and Japan. In Korea, it occurs on Jeju Island, in the central West Sea (Anmyeondo), in the South Sea, in the central East Sea (Samcheok), on Ulleungdo, and on Dokdo.

50–60 radial ribs on head valve

Narrow girdle

Tail valve

Intermediate plates

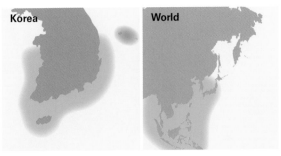

Korea

World

Ischnochiton (Ischnochiton) boninensis
Bergenhayn, 1933

EN
RA
ES
IV
T

Morphology

Body small to medium, elongate-oval. Shell plates large, elevated, notched in middle, with radial wrinkles on lateral ends. Color dark green to dark brown. Girdle narrow, ornamented with scales; about 18 fine lines present on a scale. BL: about 25 mm

Remarks

This species is similar to *Ischnochiton* (*Haploplax*) *comptus* except for the fine vertical lines on the scales of the girdle. It is usually found on rocks in the shallow subtidal zone.

Distribution

This species is commonly observed in Korea and Japan, and it has also been recorded in China (Hong Kong). Given this geographical distribution, it can be classified as a temperate species. China's Qingdao on the West Sea and Japan's south Hokkaido on the East Sea are known as the northern limit of this species. In Korea, it is found on Jeju Island, in the central West Sea (Anmyeondo), in the South Sea, in the central East Sea (Samcheok), on Ulleungdo, and on Dokdo.

50–60 radial ribs on head valve

Narrow girdle, 18 longitudinal lines on scale

10 radial ribs

Tail valve

Clear fan shape in middle of intermediate plates

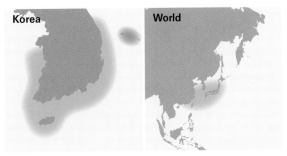

Korea

World

Lepidozona coreanica (Reeve, 1874)

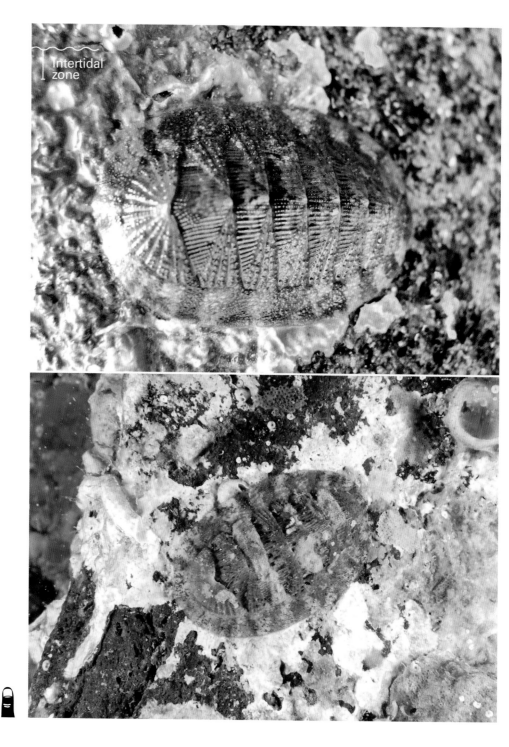

Intertidal zone

EN
RA
ES
IV
T

Morphology

Body medium, ovate. Color greenish-chestnut to brown. Shell plates elevated in middle, with regular longitudinal wrinkles. Horizontal lines present between wrinkles. Both ends of plates bearing 3-4 radial lines of granules. Girdle scale-shaped; about 20 fine lines present on scale. BL: over 30 mm

Remarks

This species lives on rocks from the middle or lower intertidal zone to the shallow subtidal zone. Compared to the two previously described chitons, the radially arranged granules and longitudinal lines at the center of the shell plates are more conspicuous and thicker.

Distribution

This species is commonly found in Korea and Japan, and it has also been recorded in Taiwan and China (Hong Kong). It is a temperate species; Japan (Hokkaido's west coast) is known as its northern limit. In Korea, it is found on Jeju Island, in the central West Sea (Deokjeokdo), in the South Sea, in the northern East Sea (Gangneung), on Ulleungdo, and on Dokdo.

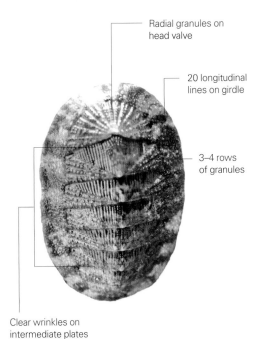

Radial granules on head valve

20 longitudinal lines on girdle

3–4 rows of granules

Clear wrinkles on intermediate plates

Korea

World

Placiphorella stimpsoni (Gould, 1859)

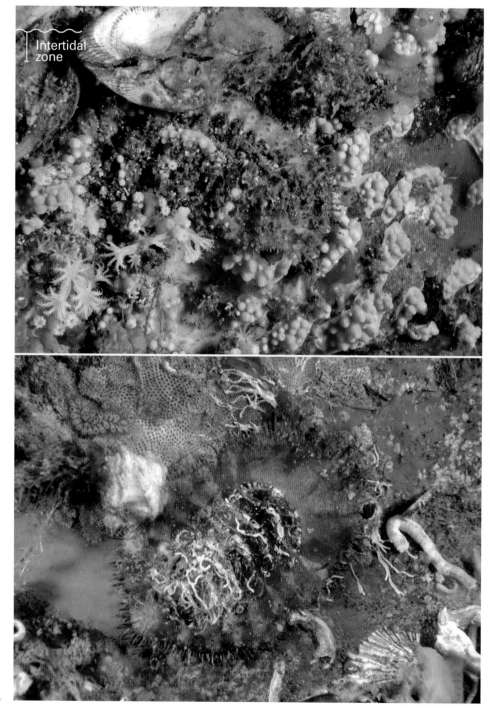

Intertidal zone

EN
RA
ES
IV
T

Morphology

Body almost circular. Girdle wider at head, narrower toward tail. Color black, brown, blue-green, purple, to apricot on valves. Head valve crescent-shaped, small, low, inverted triangle. Girdle with glassy, short, thick and irregular hairs; color yellow, brown, purple to black. Underside beige in color. Mantle bearing finger-like tubercles. BL: about 30 mm

Remarks

This species lives in rock crevices from the lower intertidal zone to shallow and fast-flowing areas of the shore. It is widely found from the walls of polluted port docks to clean rocky coasts. It lifts its head and waits for prey to enter the girdle; the prey is then caught using the finger-like projections at the front of the mouth.

Distribution

It is commonly found in Korea and Japan; it has been recorded from south Hokkaido to Kyushu in Japan and from China to Taiwan. It is a temperate species. In Korea, it is found on Jeju Island, in the northern West Sea (Deokjeokdo), in the South Sea, in the northern East Sea (Gangneung), on Ulleungdo, and on Dokdo.

Wide girdle on anterior side

Crescent-like head valve

Tail valve shaped like a triangle

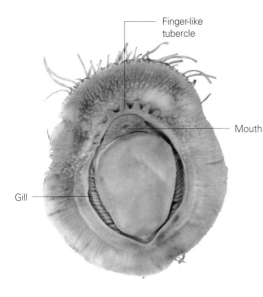

Finger-like tubercle

Mouth

Gill

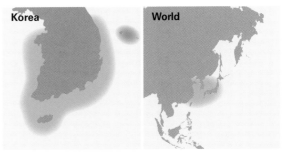

Korea

World

Mopalia retifera Thiele, 1909

Intertidal zone

EN
RA
ES
IV
T

Morphology

Body small to medium, elongate-ovate. Shell plate slightly elevated. Color black, brown, blue-green to purple. Surface occasionally covered with calcareous moss animals or other foreign matter. Head valve semi-circular, with eight lines of radially-arranged tubercles. Tail plate small, low, inverted triangular. Intermediate plates bearing two rows of radially arranged granules on lateral side; with evenly arranged pockmarks in middle part. Third plate with horizontal lines at lateral side. Girdle dark brown, with glassy and branching bristles. BL: over 30 mm

Remarks

This species is known to inhabit gravelly, sandy, or rocky shores, or oyster colonies from the lower intertidal zone to the subtidal zone. It has also been recorded at a depth of 70 m. It is commonly called the hairy chiton because it has hair on the girdle. These hairs function as sensory organs.

Distribution

It is mainly found in Korea and Japan (Hokkaido to Nansei Islands) and also in China (Qingdao) and Russia (south of the Okhotsk Sea). It is known to be a temperate species. In Korea, it inhabits Jeju Island, the South Sea, the central area of East Sea (Gangneung), Ulleungdo, and Dokdo.

Branching hairs on girdle

2 radial rows of tubercles

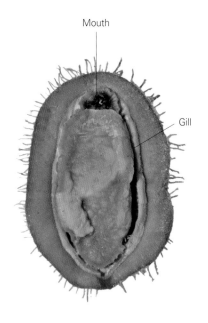

Mouth

Gill

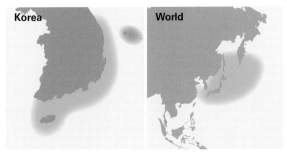

Korea

World

Chiton (Rhyssoplax) kurodai Is. & Iw. Taki, 1929

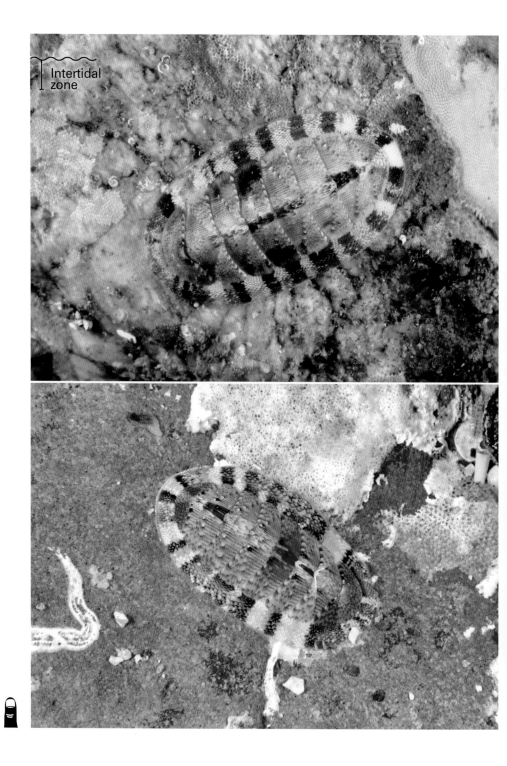

Intertidal zone

EN
RA
ES
IV
T

Morphology

Body small, elongate-ovate. Shell plates large, highly elevated, smooth, notched in middle, with regular longitudinal lines. Lateral part of middle area raised, with radial patterns. Girdle relatively narrow, neatly covered with scales of similar size; each scale bearing 16-18 densely-arranged longitudinal lines. BL: about 22 mm

Remarks

It is found mainly on the underside of rocks from the lower intertidal zone to shallow waters. It is similar to *Ischnochiton* (*Haploplax*) *comptus* and *Ischnochiton* (*Ischnochiton*) *boninensis* Bergenhayn but has less-prominent radial patterns and appears smooth.

Distribution

This species has been recorded in Korea, Japan (southern Hokkaido and Ishigaki archipelago), and China (Qingdao), and is known to be a temperate species. In Korea, it occurs on Jeju Island, in the South Sea, on Ulleungdo, and on Dokdo.

Intermediate plates with smooth stripes longitudinally

Head valve

Weak, smooth radial pattern

Tail valve

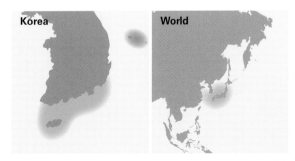

Korea

World

Liolophura japonica (Lischke, 1873)

Intertidal zone

EN
RA
ES
IV
T

Morphology

Body relatively large, elliptical. Shell plates elevated. Surface rugged, messy, covered with calcareous algae or adhesive foreign matter. Head valve occasionally with concentric growth ribs. Girdle white, black to brown, neatly covered by rounded scales. BL: over 50 mm

Remarks

These chitons differ in size and color depending on their habitat. This species is mainly found on or under rocks or in rock crevices in the middle or lower intertidal zones or live in groups along with black barnacles. In local areas around the southern West Sea or the South Sea in Korea, it is often eaten as a side dish after the shell plates and girdle have been removed.

Distribution

It is a temperate species extending from Korea, south Hokkaido and Kyushu in Japan to China. Its northern limit is known to be Qingdao in China on the West Sea and southern Hokkaido in Japan on the East Sea. In Korea, it occurs on Jeju Island, in the southern West Sea, in the South Sea, in the East Sea, on Ulleungdo, and on Dokdo.

Growth lines head valve

Rounded and blunt scales

Rugged intermediate plates

Growth lines appearing on tail valve

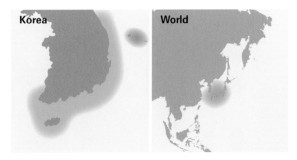

Korea

World

Onithochiton hirasei Pilsbry, 1901

2 m depth

EN
RA
ES
IV
T

Morphology

Body medium, elongate-oval. Color green or brown. Surface of plates smooth, glossy, with concentric growth lines and radially arranged black dots; head valve bearing 9-12 lines of black dots, other plates having 1 line stretching to lateral sides from center. Girdle white, black to brown in color, without scales or spines. BL: to 50 mm

Remarks

This species mainly inhabits the shallow shores of the lower intertidal and subtidal zones. This is the only species from the genus *Onithochiton* that is present in Korea. It is usually found in areas with clean water such as Jeju Island and Ulleungdo.

Distribution

It is a temperate species occurring mainly in Korea and Japan (from the southern Boso Peninsula to Kyushu). Japan's Boso Peninsula is known to be its northern limit. In Korea, it is distributed on Jeju Island, in the southern West Sea, in the South Sea, in the southern East Sea (Ulsan), on Ulleungdo, and on Dokdo.

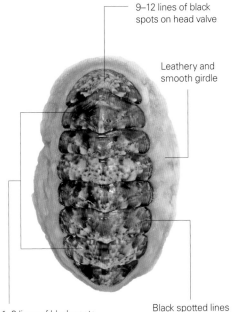

9–12 lines of black spots on head valve

Leathery and smooth girdle

1–2 lines of black spots on intermediate valves

Black spotted lines

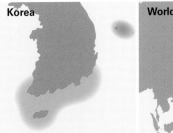

Korea

World

Acanthochitona circellata
(A. Adams & Reeve MS, Reeve, 1847)

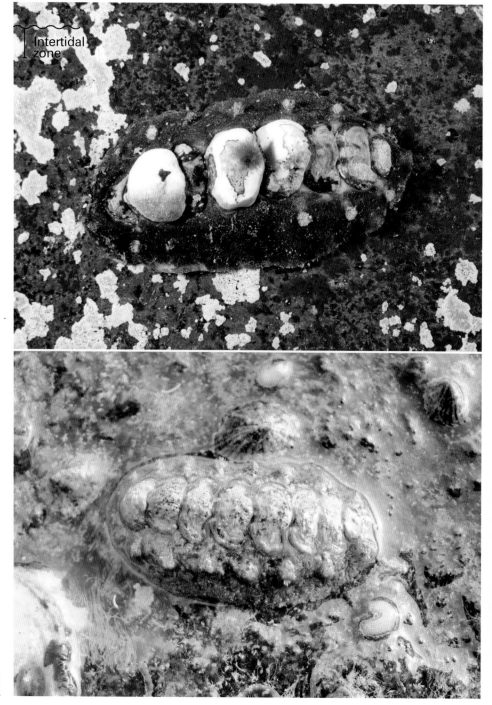

Intertidal zone

EN
RA
ES
IV
T

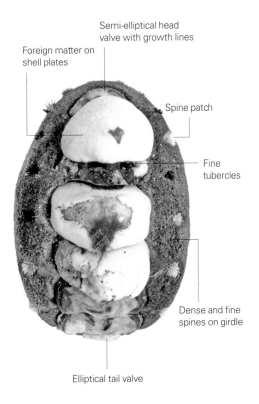

Foreign matter on shell plates

Semi-elliptical head valve with growth lines

Spine patch

Fine tubercles

Dense and fine spines on girdle

Elliptical tail valve

Morphology

Body small to medium, elliptical. Shell plate bearing fine granules. Surface mostly covered with crustos coralline algae and moss animal. Head valve semi-elliptical; intermediate valves trapezoidal; tail plate semi-circular. Girdle wide at lateral sides, covered with small spines and 9 pairs of spine patches. Color of patches white, nutbrown to brown. BL: to 30 mm

Remarks

This species belongs to the genus *Acanthochitona*. The main characteristic of this genus is the nine pairs of spine patches on the girdle, with the species classified depending on the shape of the shell plates and the girdle. Individual variation depends on the region, and many forms of foreign matter, such as coralline algae and moss worms, adhere to the surface, making it difficult to distinguish. This species is found only in Korea.

Distribution

It was first reported in 1847 as a new species on Jeju Island in Korea, and it has not been recorded in other countries, though there is a possibility that it may inhabit Japan's Tsushima or southern Hokkaido. Given its geographical distribution, it can be classified as a temperate species. In Korea, it is found on Jeju Island, in the southern West Sea, in the South Sea, in the East Sea, on Ulleungdo, and on Dokdo.

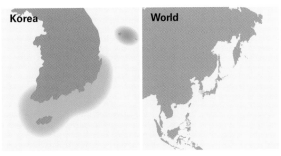

Korea

World

Cryptoplax japonica Pilsbry, 1901

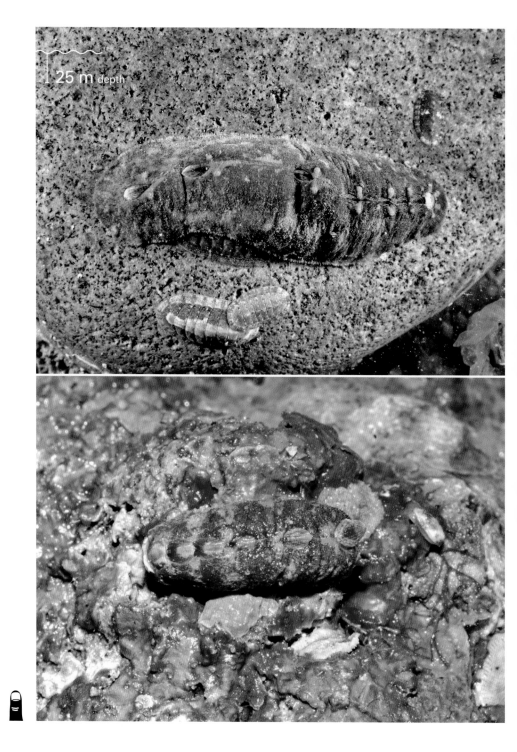

25 m depth

EN
RA
ES
IV
W

Morphology

Body relatively large, elongated-oval, with slender head and thicker tail. Color dark brown to brown, with irregular patterns. Shell plates buried, partially exposed. 1st-4th plates overlapping; 5th- tail plates separated. BL: over 70 mm

Remarks

In Korea, it is called the worm chiton because it looks like a caterpillar. It inhabits rock foundations 30 m or higher in the lower intertidal and subtidal zones. It is nocturnal and usually hides in rock crevices or under rocks during the day.

Distribution

This species is widely distributed from Sakhalin in Russia to Korea and Okinawa in Japan. In Korea, it is mainly found in areas of the ocean influenced by cold water and occurs on Jeju Island, in the South Sea, in the West Sea, on Ulleungdo, and on Dokdo.

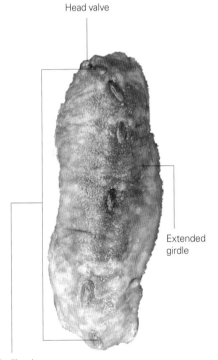

Head valve

Extended girdle

Caterpillar-like shape, covered shell plates

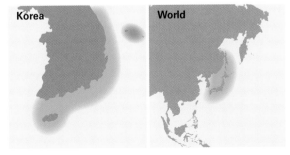

Korea

World

Invertebrates of Dokdo Island Mollusks

Class Gastropoda

Gastropoda is the most diverse taxonomic class for mollusks, with over 70,000 living and 15,000 fossil species recorded worldwide. Over 1,000 species have been reported in Korea. The head is clearly distinguished, with tentacles, eyes, a mouth, and a radula. Members of this group have a large flat foot and 1–2 pairs of gills or lungs, a nephridium, and a heart.

The primary characteristic of gastropods is the coiling and torsion of the shell and visceral mass, which was a very important event in the evolution of mollusks. The body is asymmetric, and the shell usually rotates 180 degrees with the visceral mass, though the extent of the rotation varies between taxonomic groups.

Gastropods are divided into three subclasses: Prosobranchia, Opistobranchia, and Pulumonata. Prosobranchia includes abalones and sea snails, whose gills are located in front of the heart. Opistobranchia includes sea hares and sea slugs, which have their heart at the posterior end. Pulumonata contains land snails with a pallial lung.

Haliotis discus Reeve, 1846

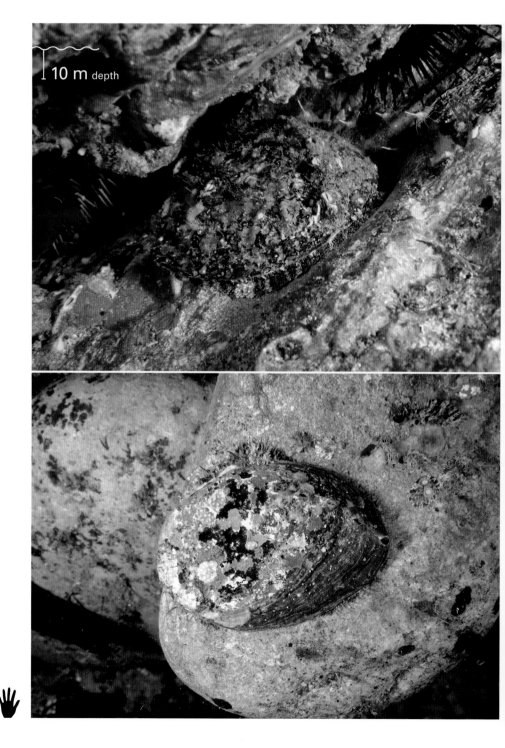

Weakly elevated apex

4–5 respiratory pores

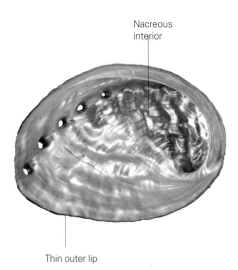

Growth lines crossing
radial ribs

Morphology

Shell medium to large, oval. Apex elevated. Color brown to greyish-brown. Growth ribs irregular, dense, rotating clockwise from apex. First spiral whorl with 4-5 respiratory pores. Inner and axial lip thick, outer one thin. Inside of shell intensely nacreous. BL: about 120 mm long

Remarks

Abalones are the most representative fishery resource for food. Abalone aquaculture is practiced on all coasts of Korea, but caging is more common in the South Sea including Wando. In Europe, this species is managed as an invasive species. *Haliotis discus hannai*, which has been observed on the east coast of Korea, is considered a variation of *Haliotis discus* Reeve that appears during the juvenile stage.

Distribution

This species is found in Korea, Japan, China, and Taiwan and has been observed on all coasts of Korea. Given its geographical distribution, it is a temperate species, with Hokkaido known to be its northern limit.

Nacreous
interior

Thin outer lip

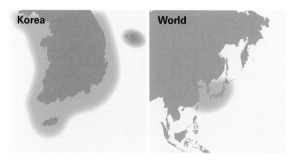

Korea

World

Haliotis supertexta Lischke, 1870

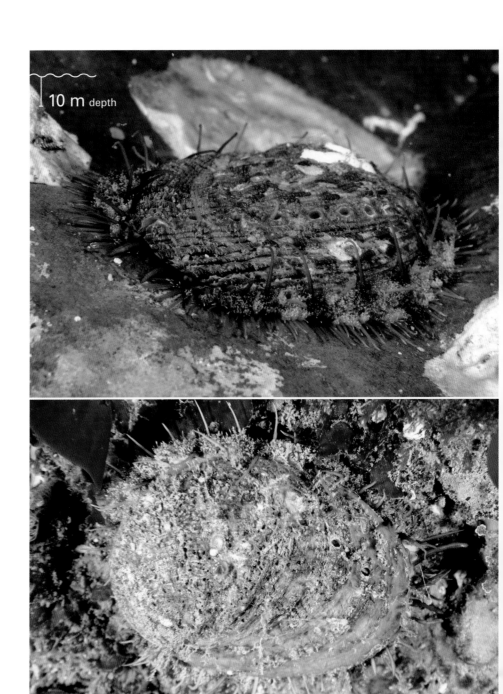

Morphology

Shell small to medium, oval, low, flat. Color reddish-brown to yellowish-brown, often with white cloud patterns. Wrinkles rotating clockwise; strong in juveniles; weaken in adults. Growth ribs thick, wrinkled, curved. 5-7 respiratory pores present, not protruding. BL: 40-70 mm long

Remarks

This species is commonly used as a fishery resource and is widely eaten on Jeju Island. It mainly inhabits the lower rocky intertidal zone to a depth of 10 m in the deep subtidal zone. In Korea, two subspecies - *Haliotis supertexta* Lischke and *Haliotis diversicolour diversicolour* - are known, but these can only be distinguished by differences in the development of the spiral or growth lines. They share the same habitat and distribution range. Internationally, the two subspecies have been promoted to species status.

Distribution

This is a southern species found in Korea, Japan, China, Taiwan, the Philippines, Indonesia, and northern Australia. Hokkaido in Japan is known to be its northern limit. In Korea, it occurs mainly in areas influenced by warm currents such as Jeju Island, offshore islands in the South Sea, Ulleungdo, and Dokdo. It has also been recorded in Gangneung and Chucksan on the east coast, but it has not been observed there recently, and it is mainly found on Dokdo.

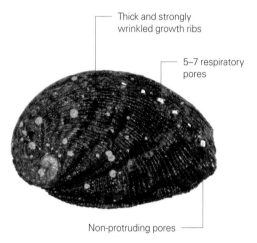

Thick and strongly wrinkled growth ribs

5–7 respiratory pores

Non-protruding pores

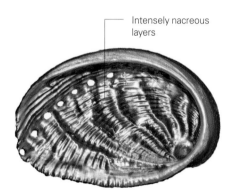

Intensely nacreous layers

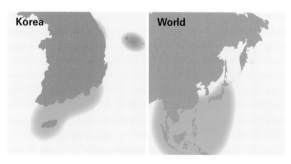

Korea

World

Tugali decussata A. Adams, 1852

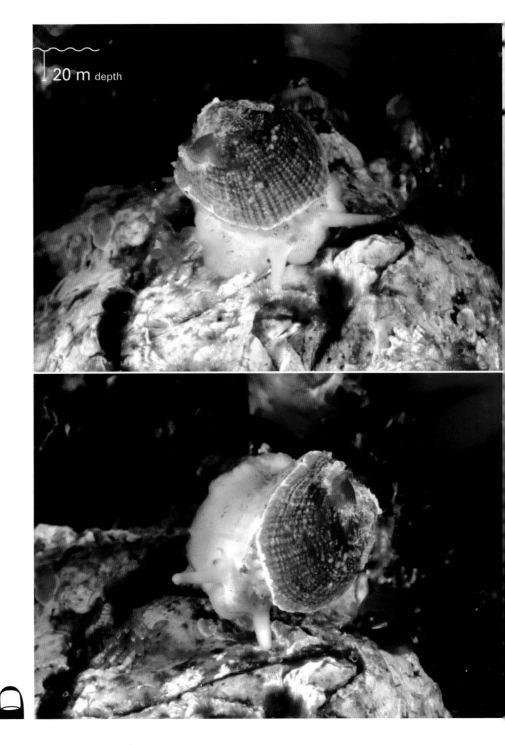

EN
RA
ES
IV
T

Apex located toward posterior, curved backward

Regular granules

Morphology

Shell white, oval, wider at posterior end. Apex tilted backward. Around 30 radial ribs intersecting with growth ribs, forming regular granules. Inside of shell white, glossy; anterior margin with shallow indentation. BL: about 7 mm long

Remarks

This species inhabits the lower intertidal zone to a depth of 30 m in the subtidal zone. It is mainly found in rock crevices, under rocks, or on the holdfast of brown algae. It is rare.

Distribution

It is mainly found in Korea and Japan. Given its geographical distribution, it is considered to be a temperate species. Southern Hokkaido in Japan and the southern coast of the East Sea, Ulleungdo, and Dokdo in Korea represent its northern limit.

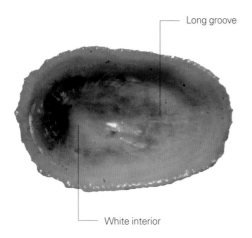

Long groove

White interior

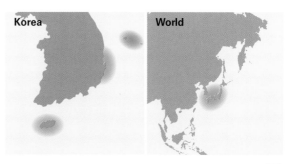

Korea

World

Macroschisma dilatatum A. Adams, 1851

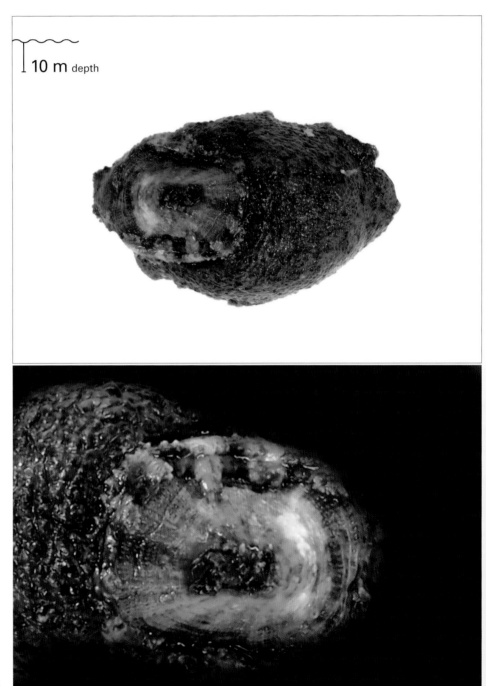

Morphology

Shell oval. Color brown, green and red in mix. Apex located posteriorly, with a long elliptical hole. Dense and regular radial ribs crossing growth ribs, forming a reticulate sculpture. Inside of shell milky white or milky blue; hole with nacreous layers (mother of pearl). Body with projections. BL: about 11 mm long

Elliptical hole at apex

Reticulate pattern

Remarks

This species inhabits rock crevices or the holdfast of large brown algae from the lower intertidal zone to the subtidal zone. Because the soft body of limpets is generally larger than the shell, which covers only a part of the anterior end of the dorsal area, the rest of the body is exposed. *Macroschisma sinense* has a flat limpet-shaped shell that is similar to this species, but it does not have projections.

Distribution

This is a temperate species found mainly in Korea and Japan (a subregion of northern Honshu). In Korea, it is found on Jeju Island, in the southern West Sea, in the South Sea, in the southern East Sea, on Ulleungdo, and on Dokdo.

Milky white or blue mother of pearl

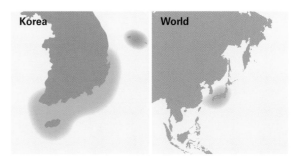

Korea

World

Chlorostoma lischkei(Tapparone-Canefri, 1874)

1 m depth

EN
RA
ES
IV
T

Morphology

Shell small, conical, thick. Color blackish brown. Spiral whorls inflated. Suture clear but shallow. Spire with 40 conspicuous wrinkles. Aperture round, nacreous; outer lip thin; inner one thick, with one denticle. Umbilicus closed, greenish. BL: about 13 mm high

Remarks

This species is commonly found in Korea. It lives on or under rocks in shallow water within the lower intertidal or subtidal zone. It has a similar morphology to *Chlorostoma turbinatum* and is distinguished by the shape of the umbilicus. In coastal areas of Korea, it is used for various side dishes, porridges, and soups.

Distribution

This is a temperate species located in Korea, Japan (southern Hokkaido to Kyushu), and (to a limited extent) China. It is found on all coasts of Korea.

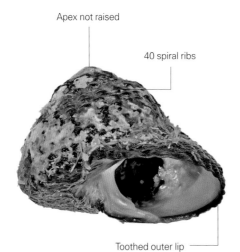

Apex not raised

40 spiral ribs

Toothed outer lip

Closed umbilicus

Green zone around umbilicus

Denticle

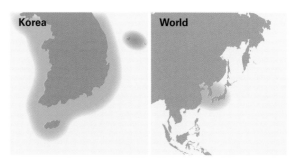

Korea

World

Chlorostoma turbinatum (A. Adams, 1858)

Intertidal zone

Morphology

Shell small, conical. Color blackish-brown. Spiral whorls convex, inflated. Suture clear but shallow. Spire with about 30 conspicuous varices. Aperture round, nacreous; outer lip thin; inner lip thick with one denticle. Umbilicus clearly pitted, greenish, surrounded by white zone. BL: about 13 mm high

Remarks

This species is commonly found in Korea. It lives on rocks in the lower intertidal and subtidal zones. It has a similar morphology to *Chlorostoma lischkei* and is distinguished by the shape of the umbilicus. In coastal areas of Korea, it is used for various side dishes, porridges, and soups.

Distribution

It is a temperate species found in Korea, Japan (southern Hokkaido to Kyushu), and (to a limited extent) China. It is found on all coasts of Korea.

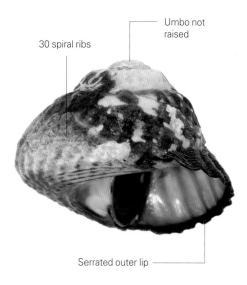

30 spiral ribs

Umbo not raised

Serrated outer lip

Greenish and open umbilicus

Denticle

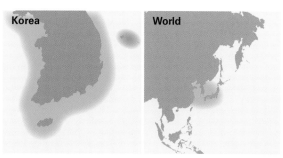

Korea

World

Tegula pfeifferi (Philiippi, 1846)

5 m depth

EN
RA
ES
IV
T

060

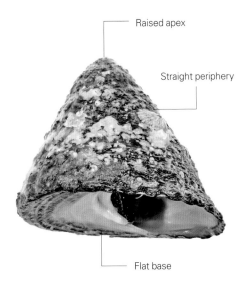

Raised apex

Straight periphery

Flat base

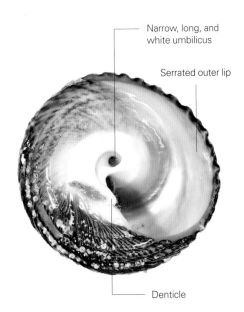

Narrow, long, and white umbilicus

Serrated outer lip

Denticle

Morphology

Shell small to medium, highly conical. Spiral whorls 7, not inflated; suture unclear; shoulder straight; base flat; periphery markedly angulated. Aperture white, smooth on inside; columella with denticle. Umbilicus coiled clockwise, profound. BL: about 31 mm high

Remarks

This species lives in clean water and is eaten in coastal areas. *Omphalius pfeifferi carpenteri* (Dunker) is a synonym that has been used in Korea, and it is distinguished from its subspecies (*Omphalius pfeifferi pfeifferi*) by the development of spiral and growth cords. However, only *Tegula pfeifferi* is recognized internationally, and the relationship between the subspecies has not been established because their distribution range and habitat are almost the same.

Distribution

This species has a limited distribution in Korea, Japan (Honshu to Kyushu), China, and Taiwan and is considered to be a temperate species given its geographical distribution. In Korea, it is found in the southern West Sea, on the islands of the South Sea, on the coast of the East Sea, on Ulleungdo, and on Dokdo.

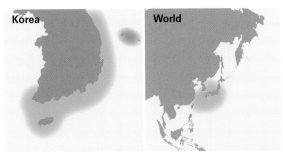

Korea

World

Omphalius rusticus (Gmelin, 1791)

Intertidal zone

EN
RA
ES
IV
W

Morphology

Shell small to medium, lowly conical. Spiral whorls 8, not inflated. Suture clear, wrinkled. Shoulder roundish, angulated. Shell base flat but weakly inflated, with greyish-brown or blackish-brown whirlwind pattern. Aperture almost quadrate; outer lip thick; inside nacreous; inner lip with a denticle. Umbilicus profound, coiled. BL: about 13.5 mm high

Remarks

This species is one of the most common sea snails on the Korean coast. It inhabits the lower (or middle) intertidal zone to the shallow subtidal zone. It is eaten in coastal regions and particularly on Jeju Island, where it is an ingredient in a well-known local food (sea snail seaweed soup).

Distribution

This species is widely distributed in Korea, Russia, Japan, China, Taiwan, and Hong Kong. It is commonly observed on all coasts of Korea.

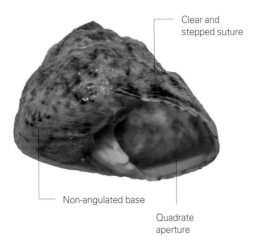

Clear and stepped suture

Non-angulated base

Quadrate aperture

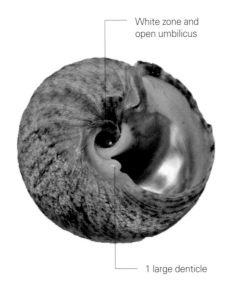

White zone and open umbilicus

1 large denticle

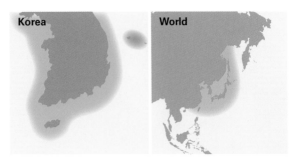

Korea

World

Cantharidus bisbalteatus Pilsbry, 1901

1 m depth

EN
RA
ES
IV
T

Round and weakly inflated whorl

Deep and clear suture

Quadrate aperture

Morphology

Shell small, lowly conical, thick, glossy. Spiral whorls inflated, convex, with irregular white spots on reddish background. Periphery obtusely angulate. Suture deep, clear. Body whorl occupying more than two-thirds of shell. Aperture almost quadrate, outer lip thin, inside nacreous. Shell base bearing 10-12 inconspicuous wrinkles, umbilicus shallow. BL: about 6.5 mm high

Remarks

This species inhabits the lower intertidal and subtidal zones to around 10 m deep. It usually lives in groups around algae colonies.

Distribution

The distribution of this temperate species is limited to Korea and the west coast of Japan. In Korea, it is found on Jeju Island, in the South Sea, on the coast of the East Sea, on Ulleungdo, and on Dokdo.

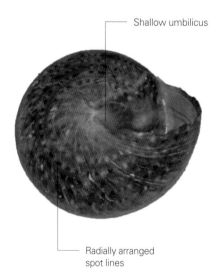

Shallow umbilicus

Radially arranged spot lines

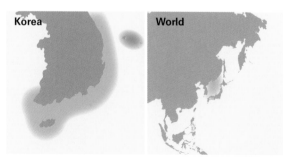

Korea

World

Cantharidus jessoensis (Schrenck, 1863)

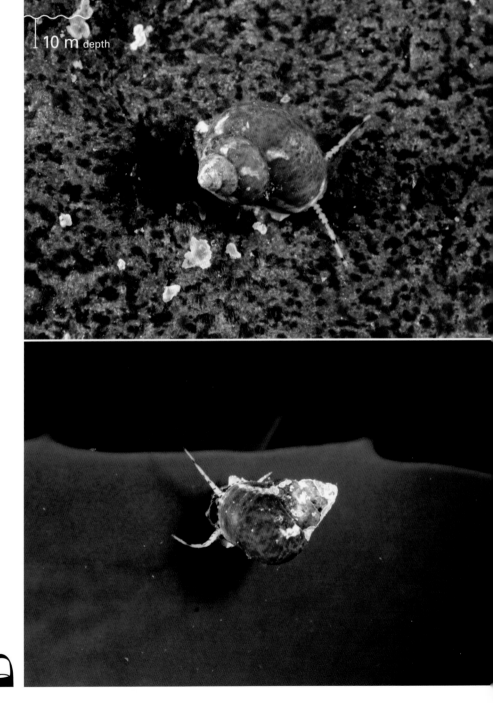

10 m depth

EN
RA
ES
IV
N

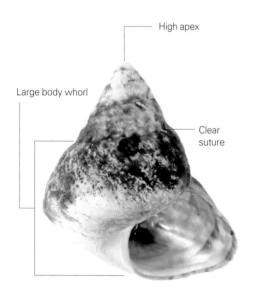

High apex

Large body whorl

Clear suture

Morphology

Shell small, lowly conical, thick, glossy. Spiral whorls inflated, convex, with irregular white spots on a brown background; periphery obtusely angulate. Suture deep, clear. Body whorl occupying more than two-thirds of shell. Aperture almost quadrate; outer lip thin; interior nacreous. Shell base bearing inconspicuous wrinkles of whirlwind shape; umbilicus impressed weakly, shallow. BL: about 12 mm high

Remarks

This species is found around algae colonies in the lower intertidal and shallow subtidal zones. In Korea, it has been recorded on Jeju Island and in the South Sea, but it is likely that it was mistaken for a similar species, *Cantharidus bisbalteatus*.

Distribution

This northern species is restricted to Korea, Japan (Hokkaido and northern Honshu), and Russia (Kuril Islands). Korea is known as its southern limit; it is present on Jeju Island, in the South Sea, in the East Sea, on Ulleungdo, and on Dokdo.

Clear spiral lines

Inner lip

Outer lip

Depressed umbilicus

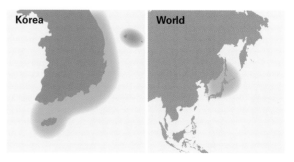

Korea

World

Cantharidus japonicus (A. Adams, 1853)

5 m depth

Morphology

Shell small, highly conical, glossy. Spiral whorl straight, with irregular white or brown spots on red background. Shoulder angulated. Suture deep, clear. Body whorl occupying more than one-third of shell. Aperture large, obtusely quadrate; outer lip thin; inside nacreous. Shell base with inconspicuous wrinkles; umbilicus pitted weakly. BL: about 12 mm high

Remarks

This species has a habitat that ranges from the lower intertidal to the shallow subtidal zone. They are commonly observed around algae communities.

Distribution

This species is limited to Korea and Japan (southern Hokkaido and Kyushu) and is known to be a temperate species. In Korea, it is found on Jeju Island, in the South Sea, on the coast of East Sea, on Ulleungdo, and on Dokdo.

Straight shoulder

Smooth and regular spiral ribs

Quadrate aperture

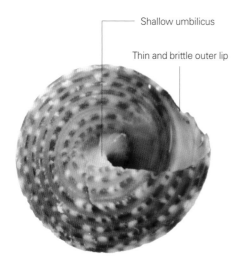

Shallow umbilicus

Thin and brittle outer lip

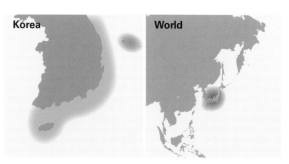

Korea

World

Monodonta perplexa Pilsbry, 1889

Intertidal zone

EN
RA
ES
IV
T

Morphology

Shell small, highly conical, thick. Color blackish-green. Spire much lower than that of *Monodonta neritoides*. Spiral whorls 5, inflated, convex, smooth, glossy. Body whorl occupying the most part of spire. Aperture large, round; inside intensely nacreous. Inner lip white, smooth, bent outward, with a U-shaped groove and a denticle. Umbilicus closed, bluish-white. BL: about 12 mm high

Remarks

This species lives on the rocks in the middle and lower intertidal zones. It is very similar to *Mongodonta neritoides*, but its spire is much lower, the suture is shallow, and the shell appears rounder.

Distribution

This is a temperate species found in Korea, Japan (Honshu to Kyushu), China, and Taiwan. In Korea, it occurs on Jeju Island, in the South Sea, on the southern coast of the East Sea, on Ulleungdo, and on Dokdo.

Spiral ribs

Large, low body whorl

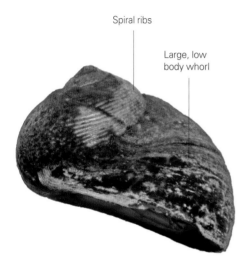

White, broad, smooth inner lip

Wide aperture

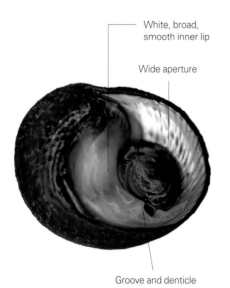

Groove and denticle

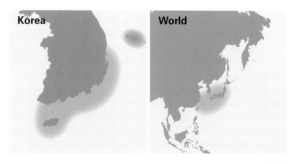

Korea

World

Stomatolina rubra (Lamarck, 1822)

15 m depth

EN
RA
ES
IV
S

Radially arranged nodules

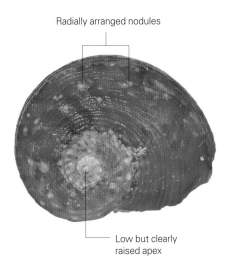

Low but clearly
raised apex

No operculum, large body

Lip

Umbilicus

Morphology

Shell small, flat, lowly conical. Color blackish-red or dark brown. Whorl roundish, broadly inflated, with white or brown nodules, stepped with clear suture. Body whorl occupying two-thirds of shell. Aperture large, circular; inside intensely nacreous. BL: about 11 mm high

Remarks

This species lives from the lower intertidal zone to a depth of 20 m (or more) in the subtidal zone and is found under rocks or in seaweed. The body is too large to fully fit within the shell. In response to an external stimulus, it severs part of its body and hides in the shell.

Distribution

This is a southern species covering Korea, Japan (a subregion of northern Honshu), China, and Taiwan. Records indicate that Korea's Ulleungdo and Dokdo are its northern limits; it is also found on Jeju Island, in the southern part of the West Sea (Gageodo), in the South Sea, and on the southern coast of the East Sea.

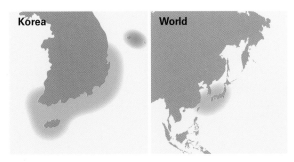

Korea

World

Calliostoma multiliratum (Sowerby II, 1875)

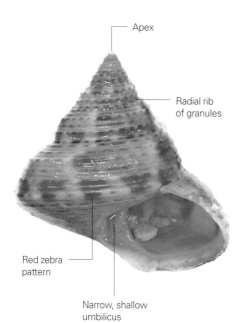

Apex

Radial rib
of granules

Red zebra
pattern

Narrow, shallow
umbilicus

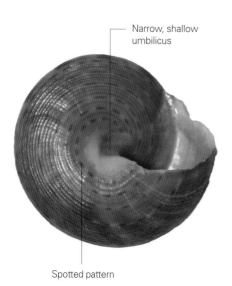

Narrow, shallow
umbilicus

Spotted pattern

Morphology

Shell small, conical, triangular, thin, solid. Apex pointed. Spiral whorls 7, weakly inflated. White and yellowish-red pattern and spiral cords leading to apex. Shell base inflated, flat. Aperture quadrate; outer lip thin with angulated bottom; inner lip white, smooth. Umbilicus closed, slightly impressed. BL: about 16 mm high

Remarks

This species inhabits the lower intertidal zone to a depth of 20 m (or more) in the subtidal zone and can be observed on rocks in seaweed or in gravel. It is similar to *Calliostoma unicum* but has some differences in its appearance, including granules on the spiral ribs and the pattern on the shell.

Distribution

This is a temperate species found mainly in Korea and Japan (Hokkaido to Kyushu). The Hokkaido region of Japan is reported to be its northern limit. In Korea, it is found on Jeju Island, in the West Sea (Baekryeongdo and Odo), in the South Sea, on the coast of the East Sea, on Ulleungdo, and on Dokdo.

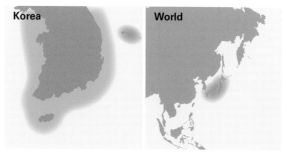

Korea

World

Calliostoma unicum (Dunker, 1860)

Intertidal zone

EN
RA
ES
IV
T

Inflated spiral whorls

Shallow spiral ribs

Quadrate aperture

Morphology

Shell small, conical, thin, solid. Spiral whorls 8, inflated. Suture deep. Irregular blackish-brown patterns and regular spiral ribs stretching from base to apex. Aperture almost quadrate; outer lip thin; inner lip white, smooth. Umbilicus closed with a shallow indentation. BL: about 18 mm high

Remarks

This species inhabits the lower intertidal zone to a depth of 20 m (or more) in the subtidal zone and can be observed on rocks in seaweed or in gravel. *Tristichotrochus unicus* (Dunker, 1860) is a synonym for this species. It is similar to *Calliostoma multiliratum* but exhibits differences in the shape of the granules on the spiral ribs, the zebra patterns, and the shell.

Distribution

This is a temperate species found in Korea, Taiwan, China, and Hokkaido in Japan. In Korea, it is found on Jeju Island, in the central West Sea, on the coast of the East Sea, on Ulleungdo, and on Dokdo.

Shallow umbilicus

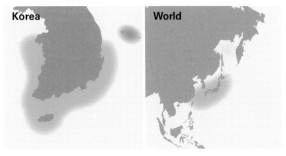

Korea

World

Homalopoma amussitatum (Gould, 1861)

15 m depth

EN
RA
ES
IV
N

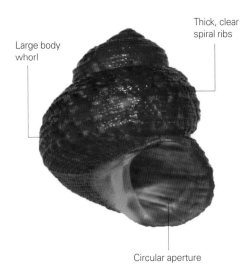

Large body whorl

Thick, clear spiral ribs

Circular aperture

Morphology

Shell small, conical, solid. Spiral whorls 5, convex, inflated. Suture clear. Body whorl large, occupying two-thirds of shell. Surface bearing thick and even spiral ribs. Aperture wide, closed, circular in shape; inside bearing wide white layers, bluish, nacreous; outer lip thick. Umbilicus closed. Operculum calcareous, with whirl-like coils on surface. BL: about 5 mm high

Remarks

This species inhabits the lower intertidal zone and the subtidal zone up to 30 m deep. It is widely observed in various places such as rock surfaces or around other invertebrates such as oysters. Three species of *Homalopoma*-*H. amussitatum*, *H. nocturnum*, and *H. sangarense*-are known to live in Korea.

Distribution

It is distributed mainly on the coasts of Northeast Asia, including Korea, Japan (Choshi to northern Nikata), and Russia, and is known to be a northern species. Okinawa in Japan is recorded as the southern limit, and in Korea, it is found in the southern East Sea (Guryongpo), on Ulleungdo, and on Dokdo.

White zone and closed umbilicus

Nacreous layer

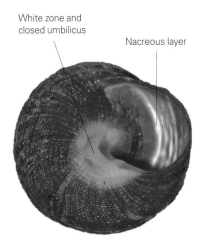

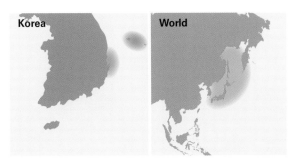

Korea

World

Granata lyrata (Pilsbry, 1890)

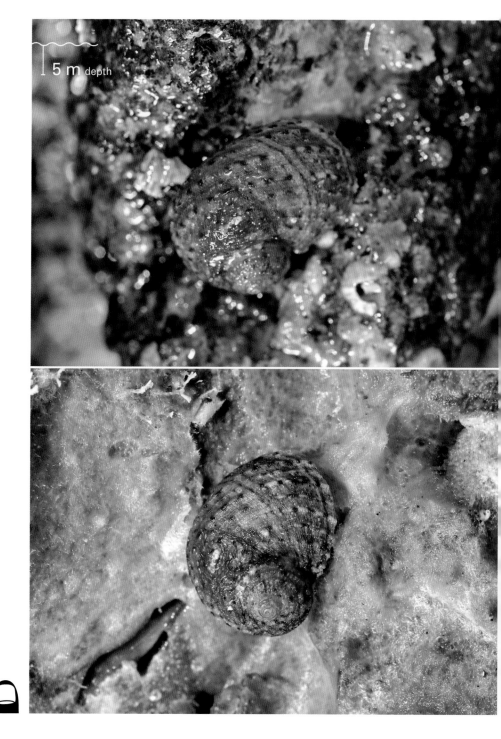

5 m depth

EN

RA

ES

IV

T

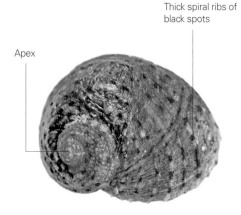

Thick spiral ribs of black spots

Apex

Morphology

Shell small, thin, flat, widely conical. Color greyish-white with black dots. Spiral whorl convex, broadly inflated, with fine growth lines between thick spiral ribs bearing black dots. Whorls stepped with a clear suture. Body whorl occupying two-thirds of shell. Aperture elliptical, wide; umbilicus small, closed. Inside of outer lip reflecting external spiral ribs, intensely nacreous. BL: about 5 mm high

Remarks

This species is found under rocks in the lower intertidal zone to a depth of 20 m. It is nocturnal and not frequently observed. Usually, around 2-3 individuals are observed on a single stone.

Distribution

This is a temperate species found mainly in Korea and Japan (subregion of Honshu to Ryukyu Islands). In Korea, it is found on Jeju Island, to the south of the central West Sea (Taean), in the South Sea, in the northern East Sea (Gangneung), on Ulleungdo, and on Dokdo. On Dokdo, it has been recorded in the southern area of Dongdo wharf and at Gajebawi Rock.

Shell

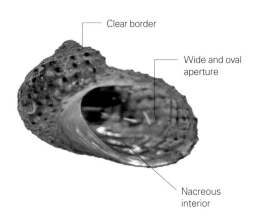

Clear border

Wide and oval aperture

Nacreous interior

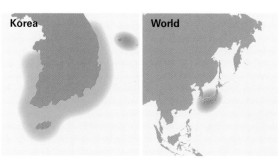

Korea

World

Turbo cornutus Lightfoot, 1786

15 m depth

EN
RA
ES
IV
S

Morphology

Shell large, conical, thick, tinted with brown or greenish-brown. Spire coiled into seven layers. Whorl clearly distinctive, large, inflated, with coarse growth lines and two rows of semitubular processes; occasionally, processes absent. Aperture wide, round; outer lip thick; inner lip widely developed, with white layers; axial lip white, thick. Inside of shell white, nacreous. Operculum calcareous, with thorn-like granules. BL: 70-100 mm high

Remarks

This species is often called the horn turban and is different from other turban shells. It is an edible species that can be farmed. It lives on rocky shores within the lower intertidal zone and in the subtidal zone up to 30 m deep. Usually, it hides in rock crevices and eats seaweed, diatoms, and organic matter on the rock surface using its radula. This species crosses its feet in order to move. *Batillus cornutus* (Lightfoot) is a synonym for this species.

Distribution

This is a southern species that has been recorded in Korea, Japan (southern Hokkaido to Kyushu), China, Taiwan, the Philippines, and the Mascarene Islands. In Korea, it mainly occurs on Jeju Island in warm currents, offshore islands in the South Sea, the southern coast of the East Sea, Ulleungdo, and Dokdo.

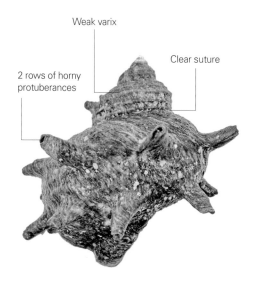

Weak varix

Clear suture

2 rows of horny protuberances

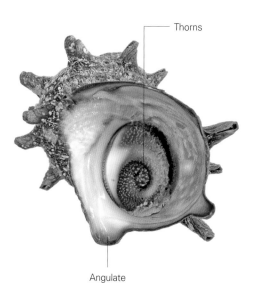

Thorns

Angulate

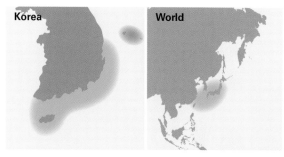

Korea

World

083

Pomaulax japonicus (Dunker, 1845)

25 m depth

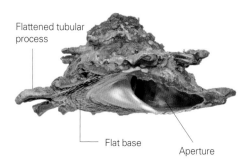

Flattened tubular process

Flat base

Aperture

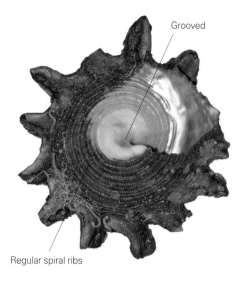

Grooved

Regular spiral ribs

Morphology

Shell large, thick, conical, almost triangular. Spiral whorls 8, with thick and wavy spiral ribs. Suture with flap-like processes. Shell base flat, with concentric and regular ridgelines. Aperture almost quadrate; outer lip thin; inside white, nacreous. Umbilicus deeply grooved but appearing absent. Operculum white, calcareous, smooth, oval, convex. BL: about 90 mm high

Remarks

This species lives at 30 m (or deeper) in the subtidal zone and is often found on the exposed surfaces of rocks or gravel. In Korea, four species of turban snails have been recorded, and *Turbo cornutus* Lightfoot and this species are present on Dokdo. This species is eaten on Ulleungdo.

Distribution

This species has been observed in Korea, Japan (southern Hokkaido to Kyushu), China, and Taiwan. Given its geographical distribution, it is a temperate species, and it is mainly found on Ulleungdo and Dokdo in Korea. It also appears on Jeju Island, on offshore islands in the South Sea, and in the south of the East Sea, but it is not common.

*Tuban snaill without processes

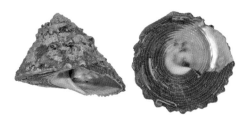

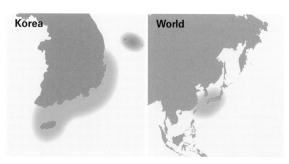

Korea

World

Cellana grata (Gould, 1859)

Intertidal zone

EN

RA

ES

IV

W

Morphology

Shell relatively large among limpets, oval, conical, wider at posterior end. Color greyish-white background with radially-arranged black spots. Apex tilted anteriorly, commonly eroded in adults. Radial ribs crossing growth ribs, creating fine and granulate sculpture. Adductor brown, owl-shaped. BL: about 32 mm long

Remarks

This species usually lives on rocks in the higher intertidal zone and is mostly found in clean water around offshore islands. It is eaten in coastal areas or on islands including Ulleungdo and Gageodo. It is used as an ingredient in limpet rice or limpet noodle soup.

Distribution

This species has a wide range that includes Korea, Japan (southern Hokkaido and Amamio Island), and Taiwan. In Korea, it occurs on Jeju Island, in the southern West Sea (Gageodo), in the South Sea, in the East Sea (Hwajinpo), on Ulleungdo, and on Dokdo. Given the geographical distribution in Korea, it is likely to be a temperate species.

Radially arranged black patterns

Completely eroded apex

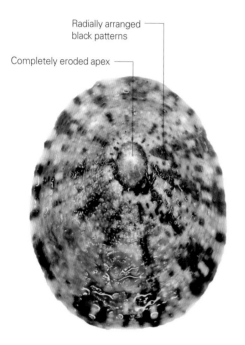

Owl-shaped brown adductor scar

Radially arranged pattern

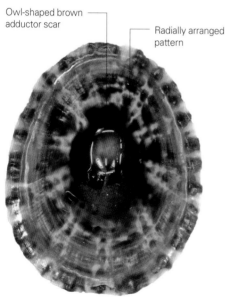

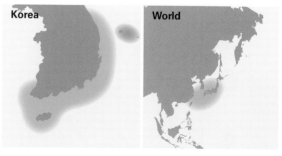

Korea

World

Cellana toreuma (Reeve, 1854)

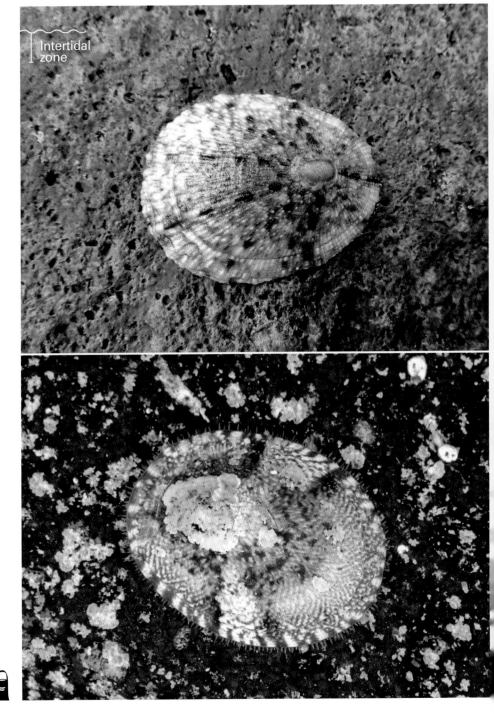

Intertidal zone

EN
RA
ES
IV
W

Morphology

Shell relatively large, lowly conical, wider and lower posteriorly. Apex tilted anteriorly, mostly eroded. Surface ornamented with irregular greyish-white or brown radial patterns. Radial ribs crossing growth ribs, forming granulate sculpture. Inside intensely nacreous, greyish-white, reflecting exterior patterns. BL: about 32 mm long

Remarks

This species lives on rocks in the middle-to-lower region of the intertidal zone. It is the most common species found on the coasts of Korea. Of the limpet species, it has the lowest shell height for its size.

Distribution

It is widely distributed in Korea, Japan (southern Hokkaido), China, Taiwan, and the Philippines. Given that the southern region of Hokkaido in Japan is its northern limit, this species appears to be temperate.

Almost eroded apex — Granules

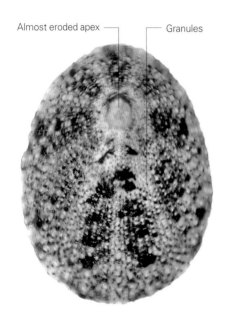

Abductor scar with unclear line, translucent, blueish milky-white

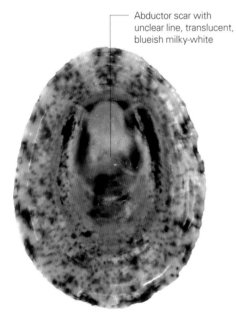

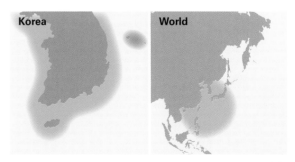

Korea

World

Lottia dorsuosa (Gould, 1859)

Intertidal
zone

EN
RA
ES
IV
W

Apex

Thick radial ribs

Layered growth lines

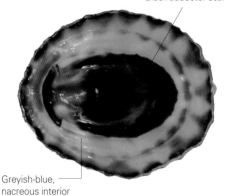

Apex

Black adductor scar

Greyish-blue,
nacreous interior

Morphology

Shell medium, conical, wider at posterior end. Apex
pointed, located at anterior end, rolled inward. Surface
ornamented with radial ribs crossed by growth ribs. Mature
individuals commonly having alternating radial patterns
of brown and yellow. Inside with deep adductor scar,
surrounded by intensely nacreous zone tinted with greyish-
blue. BL: about 21 mm long

Remarks

It lives in groups on rocks in the higher intertidal zone. It
usually occurs in higher areas than does *Cellana grata*, and
its dry shell is frequently observed during low tide.

Distribution

This species is known to be widely distributed in Korea,
Japan (southern Hokkaido to Kyushu), China, and Taiwan.
Given that southern Hokkaido in Japan is its northern limit,
it is considered to be a temperate species. In Korea, it is
found on Jeju Island, in the southern West Sea (Gageodo),
in the South Sea, on the south coast of the East Sea, on
Ulleungdo, and on Dokdo.

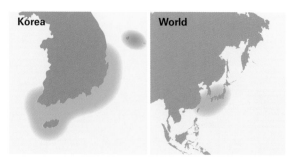

Korea

World

Nipponacmea schrenckii (Lischke, 1868)

Intertidal zone

EN
RA
ES
IV
T

Morphology

Shell small, lowly conical, oval. Apex pointed, situated anteriorly, curved forward. Surface ornamented with radial ribs and growth ribs which create fine and dense spine-like protuberances. Adults having radially arranged white spots on a brown background; some individuals of radial patterns. Internal surface tinted with milky-blue. Adductor scar brown. BL: about 8 mm long (specimen in the South Sea usually larger)

Dense spines on shell

Apex on anterior side

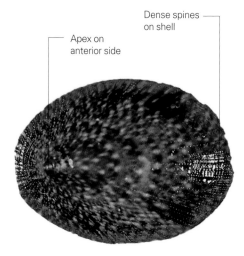

Remarks

This species is commonly found in the lower intertidal zone, usually under rounded rocks or large gravel rather than on rock foundations. In Korea, the scientific name of this species is *Notoacmea schrenckii*, which is a synonym for *Nipponacmea schrenckii*.

Distribution

This is a temperate species found in Korea, Japan (southern Hokkaido to Kyushu), China (Hong Kong), and Taiwan. It is found on Jeju Island, in the southern West Sea (Gageodo), in the South Sea, in the East Sea (Hwajinpo), on Ulleungdo, and on Dokdo.

Milky-blue interior

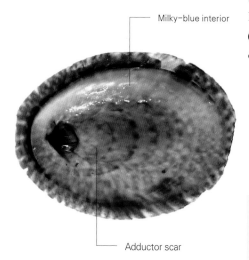

Adductor scar

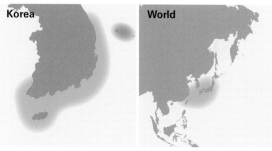

Korea

World

Niveotectura pallida (Gould, 1859)

15 m depth

Apex

Thick radial ribs

Layered growth lines

Serrated margin

Mouth

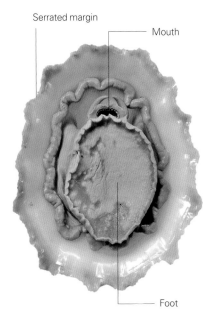

Foot

Morphology

Shell large, high conical, oval, wider at posterior end. Color white to light-yellow. Apex situated at anterior end. About 20 radial ribs originating from apex. Fine wrinkles present between radial ribs, producing a serrated margin. Interior surface white, porcelaneous, with vestigial adductor scar. BL: about 38 mm long

Remarks

This species lives on rocky shores from the lower intertidal zone to a depth of 30 m. Most individuals have various organisms attached to their shell surface, such as seaweed, barnacles, and bryozoans. In Korea, the scientific name of this species is *Acmaea pallida*, which is a synonym for *Niveotectura pallida*.

Distribution

This is a northern species found in Korea, China, Japan (Hokkaido to Toyama Bay), and Russia (Sakhalin). According to records, Taiwan is its southern limit, and it is not observed on Jeju Island in Korea.

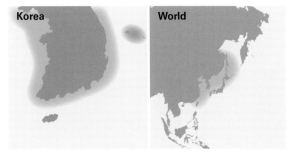

Korea

World

Crepidula onyx G. B. Sowerby I, 1824

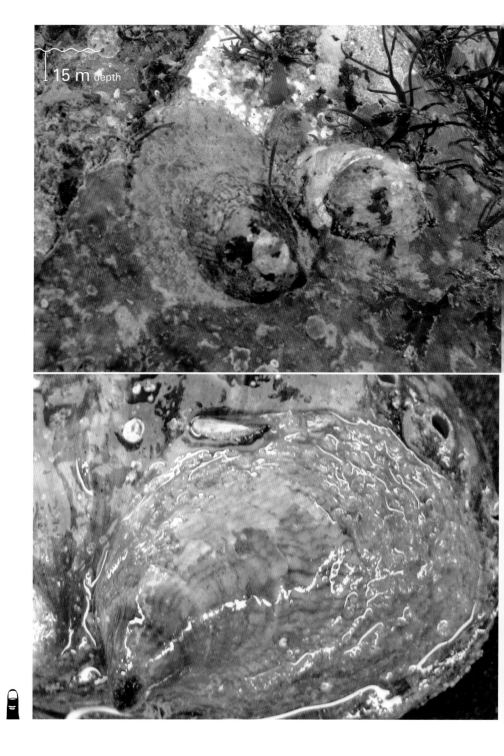

15 m depth

EN
RA
ES
IV
T

Morphology

Shell varying in size, pointed posteriorly, wider anteriorly. Surface ornamented with thin and irregular growth lines and thick radial ribs; covered with brown periostracum layers. Apex situated at posterior end, curved down toward left. Inside glossy, with a semi-transparent septum. BL: about 20 mm long

Remarks

It is found from the middle intertidal zone to around 30 m (or deeper) in the subtidal zone. It is generally parasitic on the shell surface of sea snails. It is an invasive species originating from the United States, entering the Asian region via shipments of commercial oysters.

Distribution

This is known as a temperate species due to its distribution. It is found all over Korea, China, and Japan.

Outer margin modified by the host

Thick, irregular radial ribs

Apex

Glossy interiorr

Septum

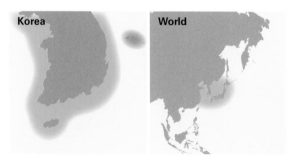

Korea

World

Purpuradusta gracilis (Gaskoin, 1849)

15 m depth

EN
RA
ES
IV
S

Black band

Apex

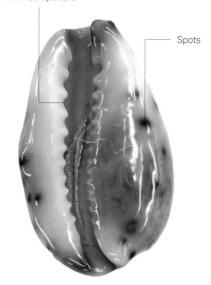

Wrinkled aperture

Spots

Morphology

Shell medium among cowry, ovate, very thick, solid. Spire curved inward. Apex rolled inward, vestigial. Surface very shiny. Dorsum yellowish-brown, with one large band of black spots. Ventral area with small, irregularly arranged spots on smooth white layers. Aperture narrow, long, wrinkled along margin. BL: about 21 mm long

Remarks

This species is found in rock crevices from the lower intertidal zone to around 20 m deep in the subtidal zone. In Korea, around 18 species of cowries have been reported; of these, only *Palmadusta artuffeli* and this species are found in places other than Jeju Island.

Distribution

It is known as a southern species that occurs in Korea, Honshu in Japan, China (Hong Kong), and Taiwan. In Korea, it is found on Jeju Island, in the southern West Sea (Gageodo), in the South Sea, in the southern East Sea, on Ulleungdo, and on Dokdo.

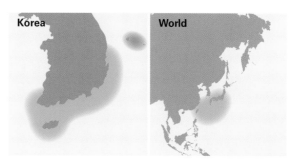

Korea

World

Littorina brevicula (Philippi, 1844)

Intertidal
zone

Morphology

Shell small, thick, almost globular. Spiral whorl 6, convex, inflated. Suture unclear. Body whorl occupying more than two-thirds of shell. Surface ornamented with thick spiral ribs crossed with fine spiral lines; 3 spiral ribs on body whorl and 2 ribs on penultimate whorl. Aperture almost quadrate; outer lip thin; inner lip smooth; siphonal canal short. BL: about 10 mm high

Remarks

This is one of the most common species on Korean coasts. It is widely distributed within the higher and middle intertidal zones, and this species often forms clusters of hundreds of individuals.

Distribution

This is a northern species found in Korea, China, Japan (Hokkaido to Sagami Bay), and Russia (Siberia). It occurs all over the coasts of Korea.

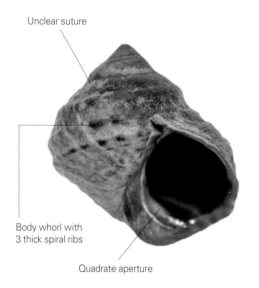

Unclear suture

Body whorl with
3 thick spiral ribs

Quadrate aperture

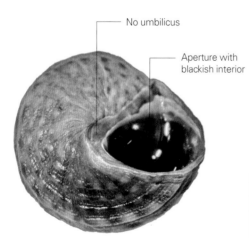

No umbilicus

Aperture with
blackish interior

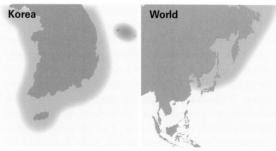

Korea

World

Echinolittorina radiata
(Souleyet in Eydoux & Souleyet, 1852)

Intertidal zone

EN
RA
ES
IV
T

Unclear suture

Dense spiral ribs of
tubercles

Morphology

Shell small, thick. Spiral whorls 6, convex, inflated. Suture
unclear. Body whorl large, occupying more than two-thirds
of shell. Surface ornamented with fine and dotted spiral
ribs of protuberances. Aperture ovate; outer lip thin; inner
lip smooth, blackish-to reddish-brown. BL: about 6 mm
high

Remarks

This species lives mainly in the highest area of the
intertidal zone and forms clusters on rock formations
that are not submerged at high tide. Prey activity occurs
when the waves strike, and most of the time, they do
not move. In Korea, the scientific name of this species
is *Granulilittorina exigua*, which is a synonym for
Echinolittorina radiata.

Distribution

Jeju Island in Korea is the southern limit of this species. It
is a temperate species found on the coasts of China and
Japan (Hokkaido to Kyushu). It is found all over the coasts
of Korea and is commonly found around Dongdo wharf
on Dokdo.

Ovate aperture,
reddish-brown margin

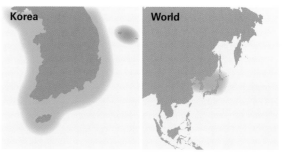

Korea

World

Hipponix conicus (Schumacher, 1817)

20 m depth

Transfigured by host

Irregular radial ribs

Apex

Morphology
Shell small, usually conical, but variable in shape. Apex pointed and curled backward. Shell base ovate, serrated by radial ribs originating from apex, with wider anterior end. Inside of aperture white or reddish-brown, glossy, solid, porcelaneous. BL: about 15 mm long

Remarks
This species adheres to the anus of large sea snails such as the turban shell or abalones to feed on their feces. The male is larger, and small females are attached to the surface around it. Given its distribution, it is considered a foreign invasive species. In general, epizoic species rarely occur at the same time in Northeast Asia and the Americas.

Distribution
The distribution of this species extends to Korea, Japan (southern Hokkaido), China, Taiwan, Australia, and the United States (West Coast, Hawaii).

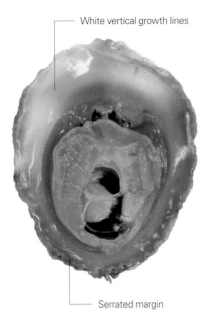

White vertical growth lines

Serrated margin

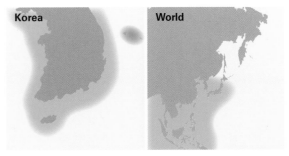

Korea

World

Sandalia triticea (Lamarck, 1810)

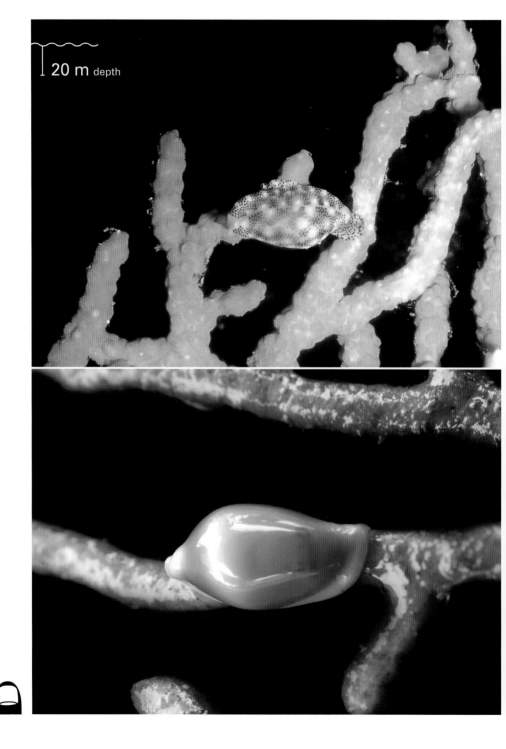

20 m depth

EN
RA
ES
IV
T

Orange, glossy surface

White vertical
growth lines

Morphology

Shell small, spindle-shaped, thin but solid, pointed at posterior end, convex on dorsal side. Color highly variable, usually scarlet to reddish-purple or yellowish-white. Surface smooth, shiny, occasionally with fine wrinkles on dorsal side. Aperture elongate, wider at posterior end. Outer lip curved inward, with around 22 wrinkles. Inner lip smooth, deeply curled inward. BL: 15 mm long

Remarks

This sea snail adheres exclusively to species in the genus *Melithaea*. In Korea, the scientific name of this species is *Sandalia rhodia* or *Aperiovula takae*, which are synonyms for *Sandalia triticea*.

Distribution

It is a temperate species found mainly in Northeast Asia, such as Korea, Japan (southern Hokkaido to Kyushu), and China. In Korea, it is found on Jeju Island, in the southern West Sea (Gageodo), in the South Sea, in the East Sea (Hujin and Uljin), on Ulleungdo, and on Dokdo.

Wider aperture

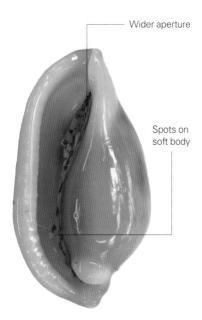

Spots on
soft body

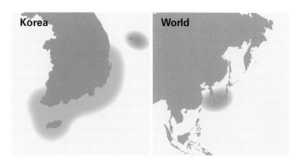

Korea   World

Thylacodes adamsii (Mörch, 1859)

Intertidal
zone

Morphology

Shell medium to large, tubular, coiled. Color greyish-brown to greyish-white. Aperture occasionally raised off floor in mature individuals. Thick horizontal wrinkles aligned consistently. Spiral ribs present. Coiling of shell variable depending on the substrate. Operculum absent. BL: 30-50 mm wide

Remarks

This species firmly adheres to rocks in the intertidal zone or at around 30 m in the subtidal zone. It secretes mucus to trap and feed on organic matter. In Korea, its scientific name is *Serpulorbis imbricatus*, which is a synonym for *Thylacodes adamsii*.

Distribution

It is a temperate species found in Korea, Japan (southern Hokkaido to Kyushu), China, and Taiwan. In Korea, it has been recorded on Jeju Island and the southern West Sea (Gageodo), in the South Sea, on the coast of the central East Sea, on Ulleungdo, and on Dokdo, but it is likely that its actual distribution range is wider.

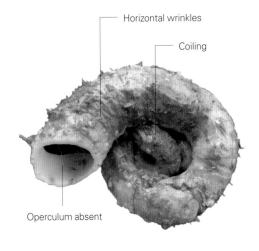

Horizontal wrinkles

Coiling

Operculum absent

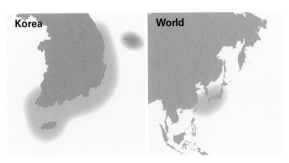

Korea

World

Monoplex parthenopeus (Salis Marschlins, 1793)

20 m depth

Morphology

Shell large, somewhat plump, covered with dark brown hair and periostracum. Spiral whorls 7, very inflated with two rows of thick wrinkles on each; shoulder angulated; suture clear. Orange-yellow or yellow-white hairs arranged along spiral ribs. Aperture bearing black stripes on inner and outer lips; stripes on outer lip more widely spaced, with around two white protuberances. BL: about 82 mm high

Remarks

It is mainly found on rocky shores at around 10-60 m deep in the subtidal zone. It is a large species but not edible. In Korea, its scientific name is *Monoplex echo*, which is a synonym for *Monoplex parthenopeus*.

Distribution

This is a temperate species found in Korea, Japan (Yamaguchi to the Boso Peninsula), China, and Taiwan. There are no records of it appearing in the West Sea of Korea, but it is known to occur on Jeju Island, in the South Sea, in the East Sea (Joomunjin), on Ulleungdo, and on Dokdo.

Black strips on inner lip

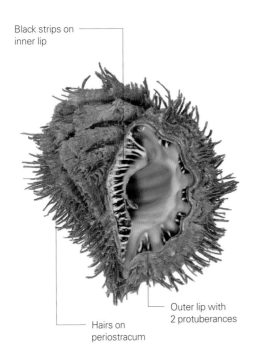

Hairs on periostracum

Outer lip with 2 protuberances

Spiral ribs

Varix on the periostracum

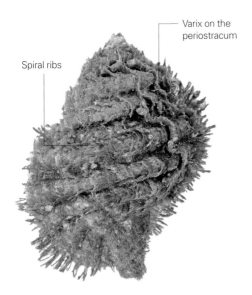

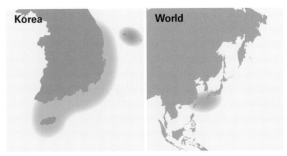

Korea

World

Reishia bronni (Dunker, 1860)

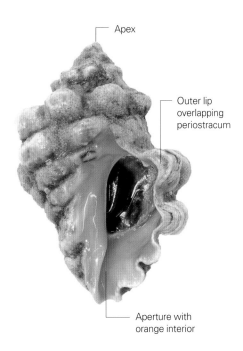

Apex

Outer lip overlapping periostracum

Aperture with orange interior

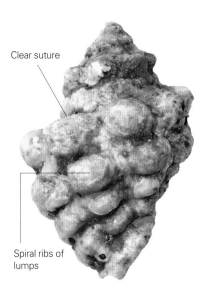

Clear suture

Spiral ribs of lumps

Morphology

Shell small to medium. Spiral whorl 6, inflated; shoulder angulated; suture relatively distinct. Dense yellowish-white wrinkles and thick lumps present over entire shell; four rows of lumps on body whorl and two on penultimate whorl. Aperture ovate; outer lip thin; inner lip covered with smooth orange-yellow layers; siphonal canal short with wide opening. BL: about 38 mm high

Remarks

This species inhabits rocks from the lower intertidal zone to a depth of 20 m in the subtidal zone, though it is most commonly found at around 10 m. It is similar to *Reishia luteostoma*, but differs in that it has yellow rounded lumps on its shell.

Distribution

This is a temperate species that has been recorded in Korea, Japan (southern Hokkaido and a subregion of the Oga Peninsula), China, and Taiwan. In Korea, it occurs on all coasts, including Jeju Island, Incheon on the west coast, and Hwajinpo, Ulleungdo, and Dokdo in the East Sea.

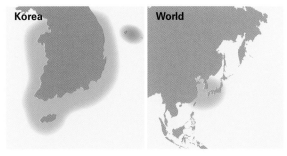

Korea

World

Reishia clavigera (Küster, 1860)

Intertidal zone

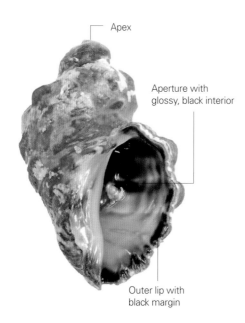

Apex

Aperture with glossy, black interior

Outer lip with black margin

Morphology

Shell small to medium, covered with small lumps. Color black to dark brown. Spiral whorls 6, inflated; shoulder rounded; suture unclear. Lumps of uniform size present along spiral whorls; 2 white threads aligned between whorls. Four rows of knob-like lumps present on body whorl; a row on penultimate whorl. Aperture of black lustre on the inside; outer lip of black margin. Inner lip covered with orange-yellow or milky-white smooth layers. Siphonal canal short with wide opening. BL: about 22 mm high

Remarks

This is the most common species found on the coasts of Korea. Its Korean name is *daesuri*, meaning "big number," due to its large population. It is used for various dishes on the west coast of Korea.

Distribution

This species is distributed widely, being found in Korea, Japan (southern Hokkaido and the Oga Peninsula), China, and Taiwan. It appears on all coasts of Korea and exhibits the distribution pattern of a temperate species.

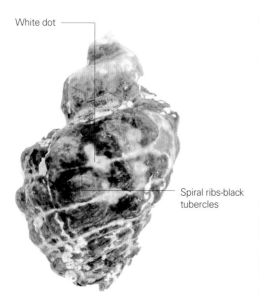

White dot

Spiral ribs-black tubercles

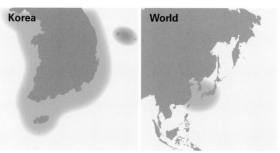

Korea

World

Reishia luteostoma (Holten, 1803)

Intertidal
zone

EN

RA

ES

IV

W

Apex

Thin, serrated
outer lip

Long, wide
siphonal canal

Morphology

Shell small to medium, covered with lumps. Spiral whorls 6, weakly inflated; shoulder angulated; suture relatively clear. Yellowish-white spiral ribs present on entire surface. Black and pointed lumps aligned along spiral whorl. Body whorl with 4 rows of lumps; 2 rows on penultimate whorl. Aperture ovate; outer lip thin; inner lip covered with smooth orange-yellow or milky-white layers; siphonal canal short with wide opening. BL: about 30 mm high

Remarks

This species lives in the lower intertidal and shallow subtidal zones. It is similar to *Reishia bronni* but differs in that the lumps on its shell are black and pointed.

Distribution

This species has a wide distribution that includes Korea, Japan (southern Hokkaido and a subregion of the Oga Peninsula), China, Taiwan, and Southeast Asia. In Korea, it appears on Jeju Island, in the West Sea (Ocean Islands, Gageodo), in the South Sea, in the East Sea, on Ulleungdo, and on Dokdo. It thus exhibits the distribution pattern of a temperate species.

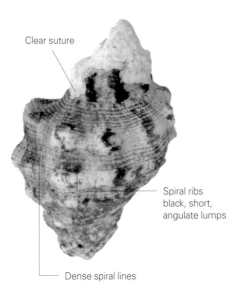

Clear suture

Spiral ribs
black, short,
angulate lumps

Dense spiral lines

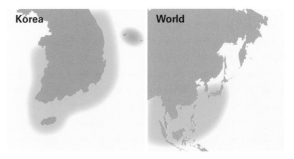

Korea

World

Ceratostoma rorifluum (Adams & Reeve, 1849)

Intertidal zone

EN
RA
ES
IV
T

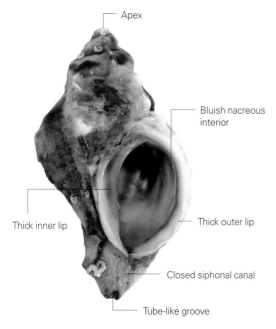

Apex

Bluish nacreous interior

Thick inner lip

Thick outer lip

Closed siphonal canal

Tube-like groove

Morphology

Shell medium, thick, solid. Apex highly raised. Spiral whorls 7, weakly inflated. Suture unclear. Varix present from body whorl to apex. Aperture ovate; outer lip thick with 5-6 denticles on the inside; inner lip with a widely open smooth layer; siphonal canal short, closed; open at tip. BL: about 40 mm high

Remarks

This species lives on shallow rocky shores from the lower intertidal zone to the subtidal zone. It is nocturnal, mostly hiding in rock crevices or under rocks during the day. It is an edible species and is called *mapsari* (meaning "spicy" in Korean) due to its taste.

Distribution

It is known as a temperate species found mainly in Northeast Asia. It can be found on all coasts of Korea, Japan (Hokkaido to Kyushu), and China.

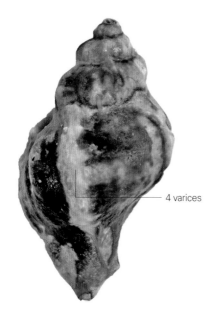

4 varices

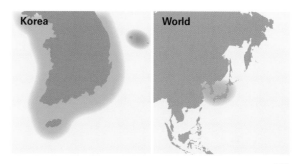

Korea

World

Ergalatax contracta (Reeve, 1846)

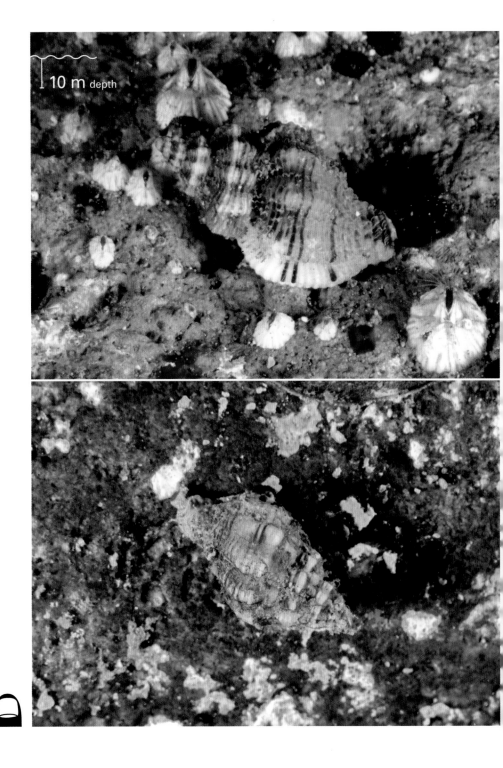

10 m depth

Apex

Thick
outer lip

White, smooth
inner lip

Short canal

Morphology

Shell medium, spindle-shaped. Apex pointed. Color white to pale yellow. Spiral whorls 7; shoulder angulated; border clearly distinguishable; suture unclear. Protuberances lined up from body whorl to apex, crossed by fine wrinkles on spire. Aperture elongate-ovate; outer lip thick, serrated with around seven denticles. Inner lip bearing wide, smooth and white or bluish-white layer, with two protuberances at middle of interior. Siphonal canal short, opened. BL: about 30 mm high

Remarks

This species lives on rocks from the lower intertidal zone to a depth of 30 m in the subtidal zone. It is nocturnal, hiding in rock crevices or on the bottom during the day.

Distribution

This is a southern species found in Korea, Japan (southern Hokkaido), China, Taiwan, and the Philippines. It has not been recorded in the West Sea of Korea, but it is known to occur on Jeju Island, in the South Sea, in the southern East Sea, on Ulleungdo, and on Dokdo.

Spiral ribs with
regular wrinkles

7 long varices

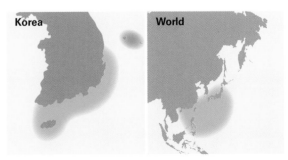

Korea

World

121

Mitrella bicincta (Gould, 1860)

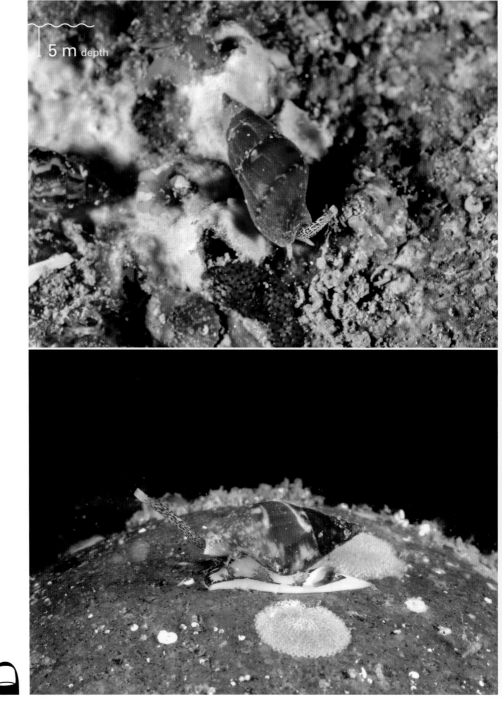

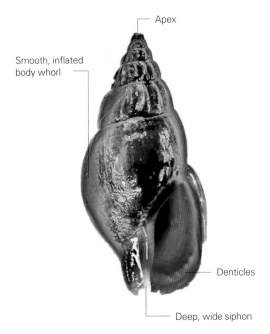

Apex

Smooth, inflated
body whorl

Denticles

Deep, wide siphon

Morphology

Shell small, spindle-shaped. Apex pointed. Color greyish-brown to reddish-brown. Spiral whorls 8, weakly inflated. Suture shallow but each whorl clear. Surface smooth, shiny. Aperture elongate-ovate; outer lip thick, serrated; inner lip with smooth, long and narrow layer. Siphonal canal narrow, short, opened. BL: about 13 mm high

Remarks

This species lives on rocks in the lower intertidal zone or at 10 m (or deeper) in the subtidal zone. It is often observed to congregate on dead fish and invertebrates.

Distribution

This species is distributed widely, including Korea, Japan (a subregion of south Hokkaido), China (Hong Kong), and Taiwan. It is found on all coasts of Korea.

Clear varix

Clear suture

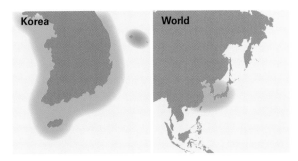

Korea

World

Nassarius fraterculus (Dunker, 1860)

3 m depth

EN
RA
ES
IV
W

Morphology

Shell small. Apex pointed. Color yellowish-brown to black stripes Spiral whorls 7, inflated, convex. Suture deep, clear. Surface smooth, shiny. Radial ribs crossed by growth ribs, producing beaded sculpture. Aperture elliptical; outer lip thick or thin; individuals with a thick lip usually having about four wrinkles. Inner lip with a smooth, long and narrow layer. Siphonal canal short, twisted, curved backward. BL: about 11 mm high

Remarks

This species lives on rocky shores in the lower intertidal zone or the shallow subtidal zone. It often congregates on dead fish and invertebrates.

Distribution

This species is widely distributed, being found in Korea, Japan (a subregion of south Hokkaido), and China. It is found on all coasts in Korea. It is mainly found in Northeast Asia, exhibiting the characteristics of a temperate species. In Korea, it is found on Jeju Island, in the northwestern region of the West Sea (Deokjeokdo), in the South Sea, in the central region of the East Sea (Uljin), on Ulleungdo, and on Dokdo.

Apex

Clear
tubercles

Black bands on
the spiral whorl

Outer lip
with one vestigial
denticle

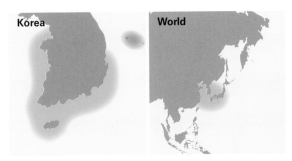

Korea

World

Engina menkeana (Dunker, 1860)

20 m depth

EN
RA
ES
IV
T

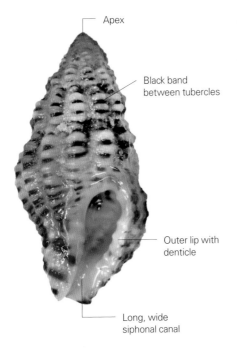

Apex

Black band between tubercles

Outer lip with denticle

Long, wide siphonal canal

Morphology

Shell small, spindle-shaped. Apex pointed. Color dark brown to yellowish-brown. Spiral whorls 7, weakly inflated; suture unclear. Radial ribs present near apex, crossed by growth ribs, forming beaded bands. Aperture elongate-ovate; outer lip thick, with around 8 protuberances; inner lip with smooth, long, and narrow layer. Siphonal canal twisted, long, curved backward. BL: about 11 mm high

Remarks

This species lives on rocks from the lower intertidal zone to a depth of around 30 m in the subtidal zone. It lives mainly on rocky shores where seaweed grows, but it is not common.

Distribution

This is known to be a temperate species that is found in Korea, Japan (the Boso Peninsula to Kyushu), China, and Taiwan. In Korea, it has not been observed in intracoastal areas; it is primarily found on islands in the open sea such as Jeju Island, Gageodo in the southern West Sea, islands in the South Sea, Ulleungdo, and Dokdo.

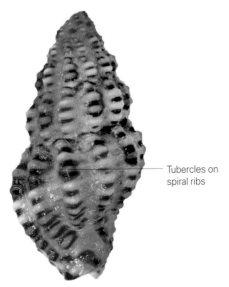

Tubercles on spiral ribs

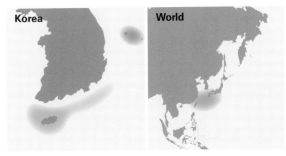

Korea

World

Kelletia lischkei Kuroda, 1938

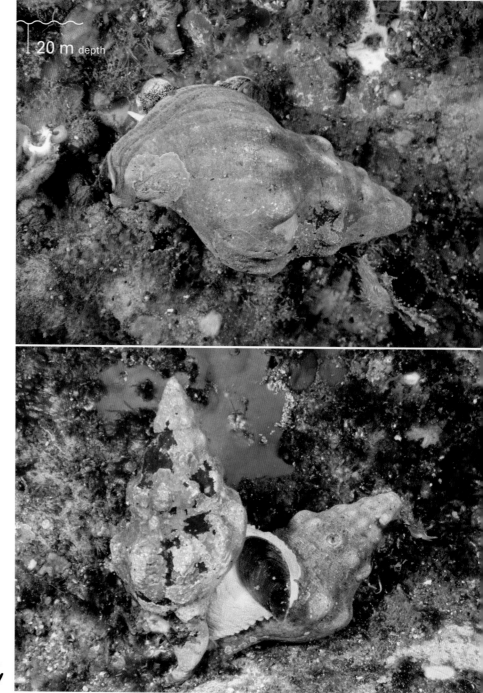

20 m depth

EN

RA

ES

IV

T

High apex

Regular varix
of tubercles

Shallow
umbilicus

Long siphonal
canal

Morphology

Shell large, thick, solid. Apex pointed. Color greyish-white to yellowish-white. Spiral whorls 8, with fine spiral lines. Suture unclear but distinguishable. Shoulder having 10-12 rows of bumps. Aperture elongate-ovate; outer lip thin, with small internal protuberances; inner lip white, with smooth, long, and narrow layer. Siphonal canal long, twisted, curved backward. Umbilicus narrow, long. BL: about 110 mm high

Remarks

This species inhabits rocks from the lower intertidal zone to a depth of 30 m (or deeper) in the subtidal zone. It is commonly eaten in coastal areas.

Distribution

This species has only been recorded in Korea and Japan (the Boso Peninsula to Kyushu). On the west coast of Korea, it occurs only on Gageodo and is known to live on Jeju Island, in the South Sea, in the East Sea, on Ulleungdo, and on Dokdo.

Regular tubercles
on spiral whorl

Clear spiral
lines

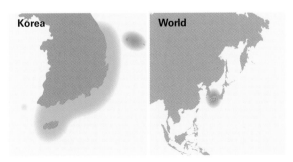

Korea

World

Pollia subrubiginosa (E. A. Smith, 1879)

15 m depth

EN
RA
ES
IV
T

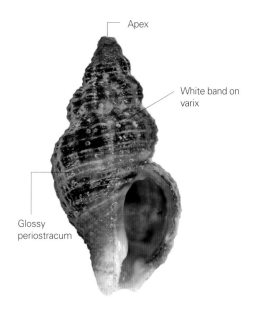

Apex

White band on
varix

Glossy
periostracum

Morphology

Shell small, spindle-shaped. Apex pointed. Color dark brown to reddish-brown. Spiral whorls 8, convex, inflated. Suture deep, clear. About 4-5 spiral ribs of uniform thickness crossed by growth ribs, forming bands. Aperture elongate-ovate; outer lip thick, with around 8 internal protuberances; inner lip white, with a smooth, long, and narrow layer. Siphonal canal twisted, long, curved backward. BL: about 20 mm high

Remarks

This species inhabits rock formations from the lower intertidal zone to a depth of 30 m in the subtidal zone. *Pollia mollis* reported in Korea is similar in shape to this species; in Korea, it is distinguished by the degree of inflation of the shell, the thickness of the outer lip, and the strength of the varix. However, it is not easy to distinguish the two species morphologically because some individuals have a mix of traits from both species

Distribution

This is a temperate species found mainly in Korea and Japan (the Boso Peninsula to Kyushu). It is most commonly found on Jeju Island in Korea and inhabits the southern region of the West Sea (Gageodo), the South Sea, Ulleungdo, and Dokdo. It has not been observed on the east coast of Korea.

Black band on
varix

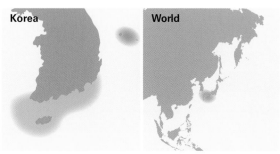

Korea

World

Haminoea japonica Pilsbry, 1895

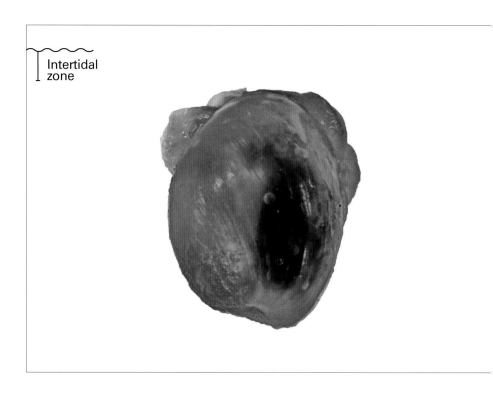

Intertidal zone

1 spiral whorl, buried apex

Thin, egg-like shell

Morphology

Shell small, ovate, very thin, translucent. Color white to yellow. Spire absent; a spiral whorl present with fine spiral lines. Aperture narrow and long at top, wider toward bottom. Outer lip thin, brittle. Inner lip smooth, wider at bottom. Body thick, brown or greenish-brown, with black spots. BL: about 15 mm high

Remarks

This species lives in clean intertidal zones and is mainly found in tidal pools with a lot of seaweed or on shallow rocky shores. During spring, it is possible to observe this species attaching its eggs to seaweed.

Distribution

This is a temperate species found mainly in Korea and Japan (Hokkaido to Kyushu). It is most commonly found in the northern region of the East Sea but also occurs on Jeju Island, in the southern region of the West Sea (Gageodo), in the South Sea, on Ulleungdo and on Dokdo.

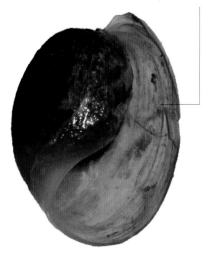

Aperture becoming wider at posterior

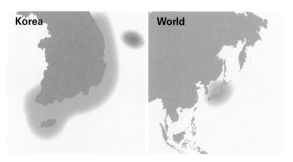

Korea

World

Elysia atroviridis Baba, 1955

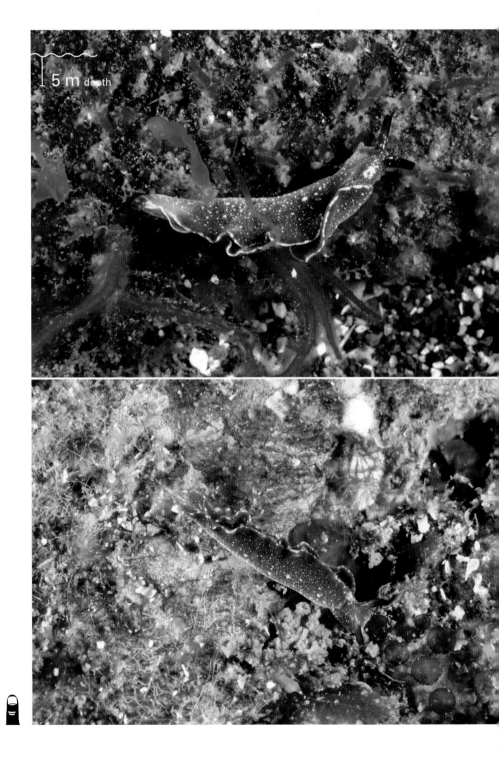

5 m depth

EN
RA
ES
IV
S

Morphology

Body small. Color translucent green to dark-green, with many white spots. Rhinophore dark blue or black at tip, gradually paler toward base. Border of parapodia lined in white. BL: about 20 mm long

Remarks

This species mainly lives in areas with well-developed algae communities (green or red algae) at a depth of about 20 m in the lower intertidal zone. *Elysia flavomacula* Jensen, which has also been reported in Korea, is the same species but is considered a morphological variant.

Distribution

This species has been reported only in subtropical areas including Korea, Japan (Honshu to Kyushu), China (Hong Kong), and Taiwan. In Korea, it is found on Jeju Island, offshore islands in the South Sea, on Ulleungdo, and on Dokdo. In Dokdo, it is observed around the Dongdo wharf.

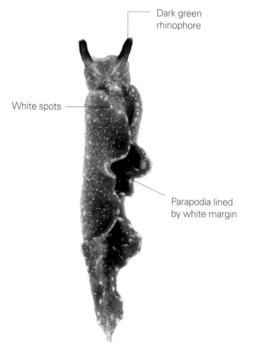

Dark green rhinophore

White spots

Parapodia lined by white margin

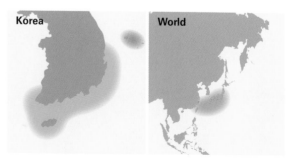

Korea

World

Elysia abei Baba, 1955

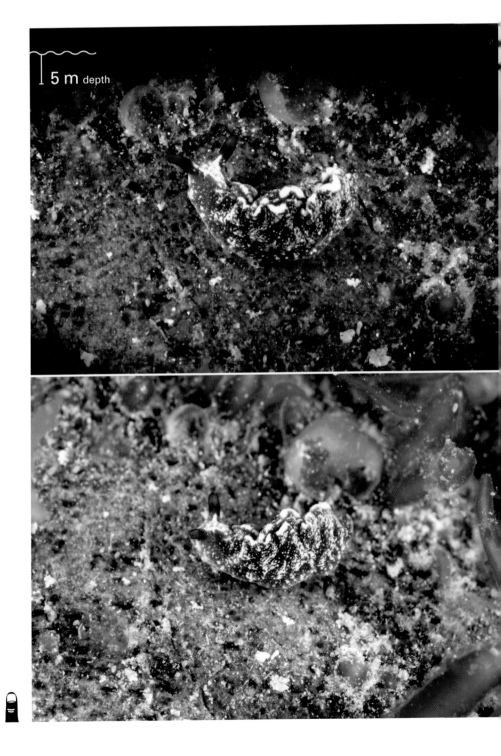

5 m depth

EN
RA
ES
IV
T

Morphology

Body small. Color light green to dark brown, with many white spots. Rhinophore dark purple at tips, gradually paler at base. Parapodia corrugated at lateral end, with white border. BL: about 15 mm long

Remarks

This species mainly lives in areas with algae colonies (green or red algae) at a depth of about 20 m in the lower intertidal zone. It is frequently observed from winter to spring when the water temperature is low. *Elysia amakusana* Baba is the same species but is considered a morphological variant.

Distribution

In Korea, this species is observed on Jeju Island, offshore islands in the South Sea, Ulleungdo, and Dokdo, and is considered to be a temperate species given its geographical distribution. It has also been reported in Japan (Sagami Bay) and has been observed around the Dongdo wharf on Dokdo.

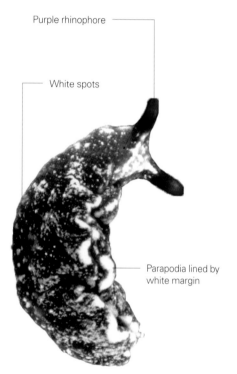

Purple rhinophore

White spots

Parapodia lined by white margin

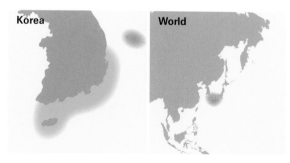

Korea

World

Aplysia kurodai Baba, 1937

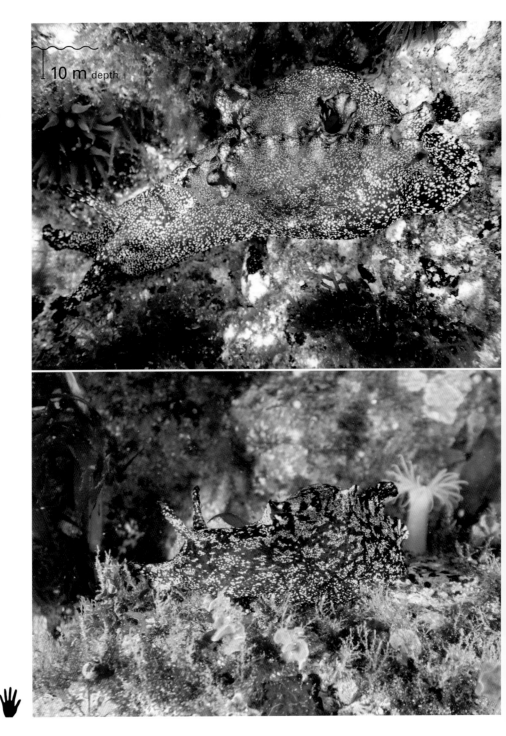

EN
RA
ES
IV
T

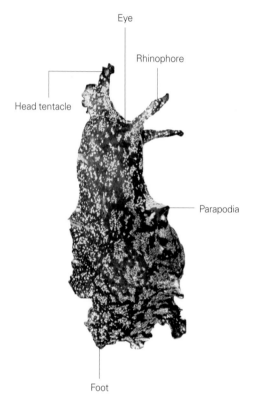

Eye

Rhinophore

Head tentacle

Parapodia

Foot

Morphology

Body large. Color black or dark brown, with irregular white spots over entire body except for foot. Elongated neck present behind head. Body under neck largely inflated, slender at foot. Head with a pair of tentacles, rhinophores, and eyes, respectively. Parapodia on lateral side covering visceral mass and mantle on dorsal side. Shell flat, oval, translucent brown, covered by mantle. BL: 150-300 mm long

Remarks

This species mainly lives in areas where algae colonies (green or red algae) are common in the lower intertidal zone to a depth of about 20 m. It is found frequently from late winter to early summer and mates in groups, usually in late spring. When stimulated or threatened, dark purple secretions of ink are released. It is eaten as a side dish on the south and east coasts of Korea.

Distribution

This is a temperate species found in Korea, Japan (southern Hokkaido to Kyushu), China, and Taiwan. It is commonly observed on all coasts of Korea and has been found in most regions of Dokdo, including Dongdo and Seodo and Gajebawi Rock.

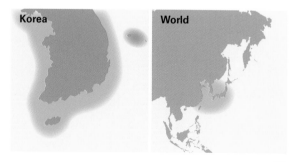

Korea

World

Aplysia juliana Quoy & Gaimard, 1832

5 m depth

EN
RA
ES
IV
W

Morphology

Body large, very inflated. Color light brown, with milky and irregular spots over entire body except for foot. Head forming a long and slender neck, with 2 tentacles, rhinophores, and eyes, respectively. Posterior end of foot forming a sucker that can act as anchor. Parapodia on lateral side covering visceral mass and mantle on dorsal side, connected at posterior end. BL: 200-450 mm long

Remarks

This species mainly lives in the lower intertidal zone to a depth of 20 m where algae colonies (green or red algae) are present. It is found frequently from winter to spring when the water temperature is low and mates in groups, usually in late spring. When stimulated or threatened, it releases a milky secretion. It is very similar to *Aplysia kurodai* Baba, but its base color is not black, it has a sucker at the posterior end of the foot, and its parapodia are connected at the posterior end.

Distribution

This species is widely distributed in subtropical and temperate regions around the world, including Korea, Japan (a subregion of Honshu), China, Taiwan, the Indian Ocean, the Atlantic Ocean, and the African coast. In Korea, it has been observed on Jeju Island, in the western region of the West Sea (Gageodo), in the South Sea, in the southern region of the East Sea, on Ulleungdo, and on Dokdo. It is found all over the Dokdo coast.

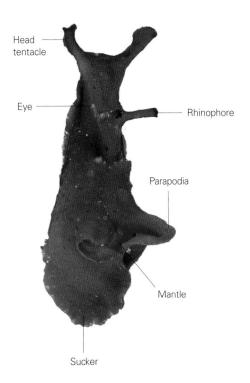

Head tentacle

Eye

Rhinophore

Parapodia

Mantle

Sucker

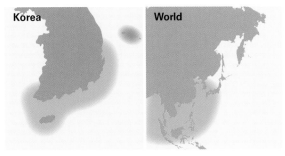

Korea

World

Aplysia parvula Mörch, 1863

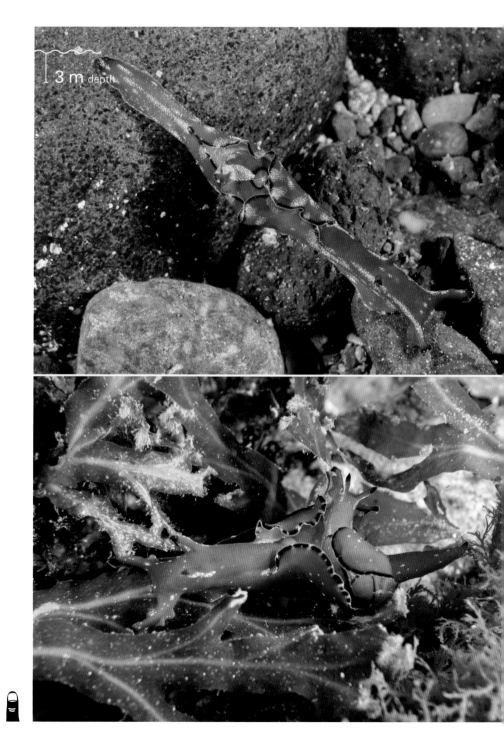

3 m depth

EN
RA
ES
IV
S

Morphology

Body small to medium, very inflated. Color dark brown, with milky and irregular spots except for foot. Head and parapodia having dark brown or black margins. Head forming a slender and long neck, with tentacles, rhinophores, and eyes, respectively. Parapodia on lateral side covering visceral mass and mantle on dorsal side. BL: about 60 mm long

Remarks

This species mainly inhabits the lower intertidal zone to a depth of 20 m where algae colonies are found. It is frequently observed from winter to spring when the water temperature is low and mates in groups, usually in late spring. When stimulated or threatened, it releases dark purple secretions or ink, as with *Aplysia kurodai* Baba.

Distribution

This species is found worldwide, including in Korea, Japan (a subregion of Honshu), China, Taiwan, the Indian Ocean, Australia, the United States (West Coast, Hawaii), the southern coast of Africa, and the Mediterranean. In Korea, it is mainly found on Jeju Island, in the sub-central region of the West Sea, in the South Sea, in the sub-central region of the East Sea, on Ulleungdo, and on Dokdo. It is found all over the Dokdo coast.

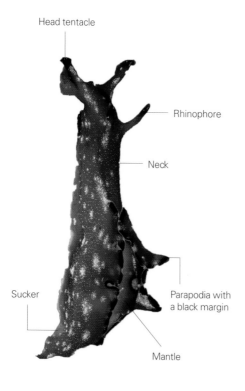

Head tentacle

Rhinophore

Neck

Sucker

Parapodia with a black margin

Mantle

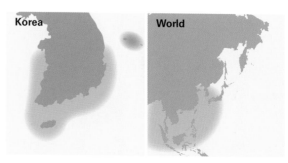

Korea

World

Pleurobranchaea japonica Thiele, 1925

Morphology

Body medium, flat. Color light brown, with irregular net-like patterns. Shell absent. Mouth cylindrical, located under head shield. Head shield widened outward, reverse quadrilateral. Rhinophore curled outward with open tip. Gill located under right mantle skirt, spreading up and down. Foot spreading widely, larger than mantle, pointed at posterior end, externally exposed. BL: 50-110 mm long

Remarks

This species inhabits rocks from the lower intertidal zone to a depth of 30 m. When stimulated or threatened, it floats and swims on the surface of the water by repeatedly folding and unfolding its body. Typically, its population density is not high, but individuals will congregate during the breeding season.

Distribution

This species is found in Korea, Japan (Honshu to Kyushu), China (Qingdao, Bohai), and New Zealand. It is found on all coasts of Korea and over the entire coast of Dokdo.

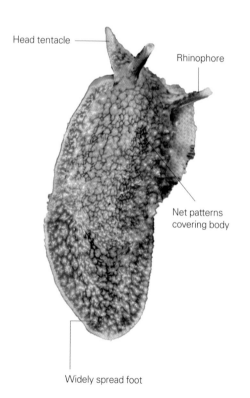

Head tentacle

Rhinophore

Net patterns covering body

Widely spread foot

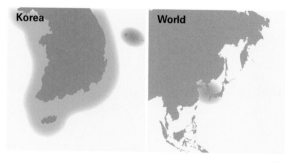

Korea

World

Berthellina citrina (Rüppell & Leuckart, 1828)

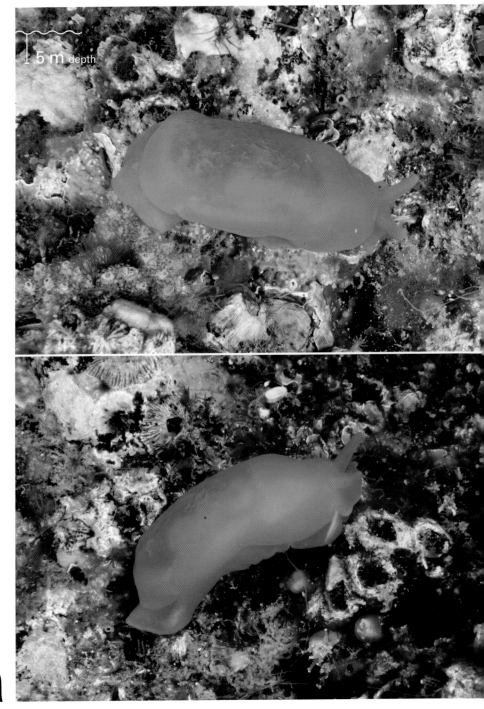

5 m depth

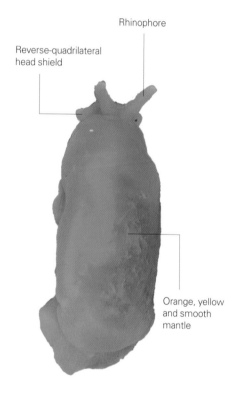

Reverse-quadrilateral
head shield

Rhinophore

Orange, yellow
and smooth
mantle

Morphology

Body small to medium, hemispherical. Color light orange to yellow. Gill located under right mantle skirt. Surface of mantle smooth. Mouth located between head shield and foot. Head reverse-quadrilateral. Rhinophores cylindrical, connected at base. Anus located in middle. About 25 feather-like gills spreading up and down. Genital pore present in front of gills; male genitalia looking like a hook with pointed tip. BL: about 40 mm long

Remarks

It inhabits rock formations from the lower subtidal zone to a depth of 30 m. It often hides in the substrate of large brown algae species such as *E. bicyclis* and *E. cava*.

Distribution

This species has a wide distribution, being found in tropical, subtropical, and temperate regions, including Korea, Japan (Wakashi Bay to Sagami Bay), China, Polynesia, Galapagos, the USA (California Coast, Hawaii), southern England, Indonesia, southern Africa, Madagascar, the Mediterranean Sea, and the Red Sea. In Korea, it is rarely found on Jeju Island, in the southern West Sea (Gageodo), and on offshore islands in the South Sea. However, it is relatively common in the southern East Sea, on Ulleungdo, and on Dokdo.

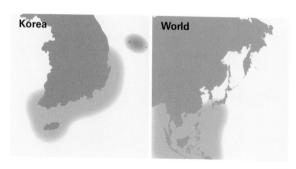

Korea

World

Okenia hiroi (Baba, 1938)

10 m depth

Morphology

Body very small. Color pinkish. Head, foot and mantle merged into one, not distinguishable. Elongated papillae distributed over entire mantle. Pink color turning pale at papillae tip. Rhinophores looking like feather arranged left and right. About 3-5 petal-like gills located in front of anus. BL: about 5 mm long

Remarks

This species inhabits rocks or rock crevices from the lower subtidal zone to a depth of about 30 m. It is often observed around red-colored moss animals.

Distribution

This species has a distribution from Korea and southern Hokkaido in Japan to China (Hong Kong). In Korea, it is found on Jeju Island, the offshore islands in the South Sea, Ulleungdo, and Dokdo. It has been observed on Gajebawi Rock and the annexed islands in front of Seodo on Dokdo.

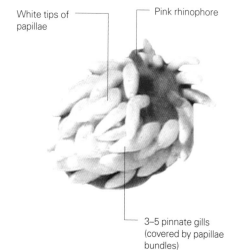

White tips of papillae — Pink rhinophore

3–5 pinnate gills (covered by papillae bundles)

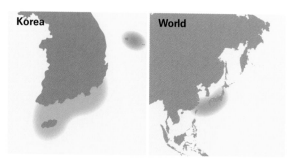

Korea   World

Platydoris ellioti (Alder & Hancock, 1864)

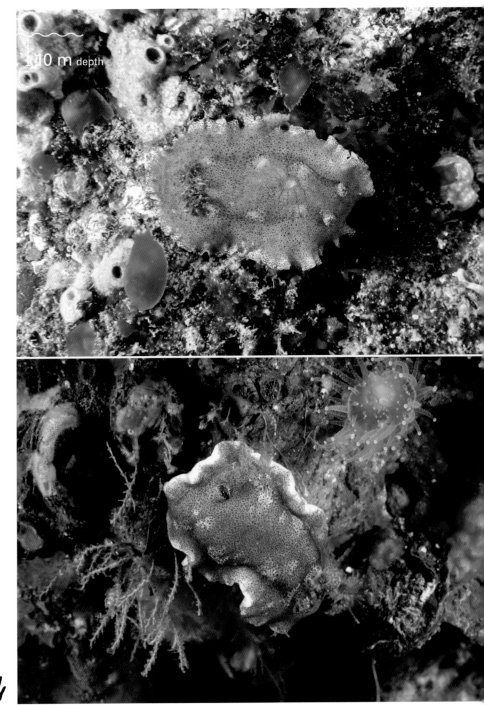

EN
RA
ES
IV
S

Morphology

Body medium, oval, flat. Color dark brown to orange, with milky white spots on dorsum. Rhinophore and gill sheaths raised higher than mantle. Gill having 6 lobes. Mantle wrinkled at margin, with bands of light brown spots. Foot and mantle yellow or light orange at underside. Mantle with dark brown spots. BL: over 70 mm long

Remarks

This species lives under rocks or in rock crevices from the lower intertidal zone to a depth of about 20 m. Because it camouflages itself with colors similar to the surrounding environment, it is difficult to observe. In Korea, the scientific name of this species is *Platydoris speciosa* (Abraham), which is a synonym for *Platydoris ellioti*.

Distribution

It is widely distributed across tropical and subtropical regions of the Indo-Pacific coast, such as Korea, Japan (a subregion of the Noto Peninsula to the Boso Peninsula), China, Taiwan, and the Philippines. In Korea, it is found on Jeju Island, offshore islands of the South Sea, Ulleungdo, and Dokdo. On Dokdo, it has been observed on Gajebawi Rock and Dongdo.

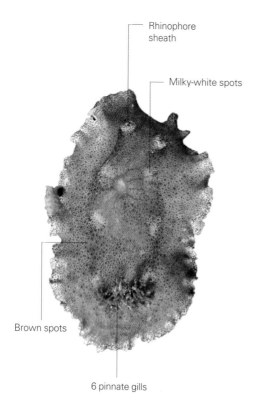

Rhinophore sheath

Milky-white spots

Brown spots

6 pinnate gills

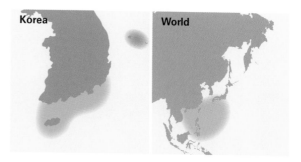

Korea

World

Cadlina japonica Baba, 1937

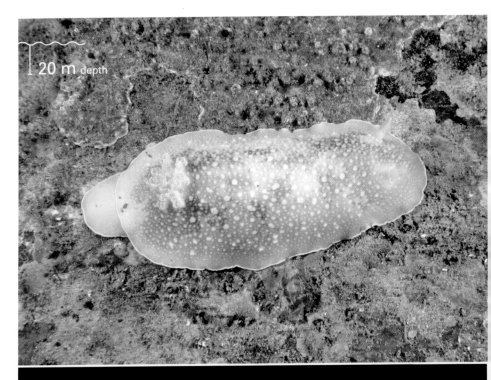

20 m depth

EN
RA
ES
IV
N

Morphology

Body medium, oval, flat. Color light brown to beige. Margin lined by thin yellow band. Rounded tubercles covering dorsum. Mantle skirt covering body. Posterior tip of foot projecting out. Mouth divided laterally, with oral tentacles. Rhinophore pinnately compound. Rhinophore and its sheath also having dark color along edges. Six gills tripinnate, surrounding anus, bordered by dark color. BL: 30-70 mm long

Remarks

This species lives under rocks or in rock crevices from the lower intertidal zone to a depth of about 20 m. Though its body color can vary, it is pale-brown or beige in most cases. It is commonly found on the east coast of Korea, especially on Dokdo and Ulleungdo.

Distribution

This species is found in Korea, Japan (Hokkaido to Honshu), and Bohai Bay in China. In Korea, it has been observed on Jeju Island, in the southern West Sea (Gageodo), in the South Sea (Chujado), on the coast of the East Sea, on Ulleungdo, and on Dokdo. It has the characteristics of a northern species, and Japan's Kii Peninsula and the offshore islands of Korea represent its southern limit.

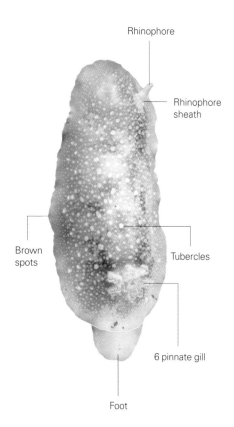

Rhinophore

Rhinophore sheath

Brown spots

Tubercles

6 pinnate gill

Foot

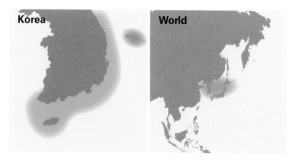

Korea

World

Homoiodoris japonica Bergh, 1882

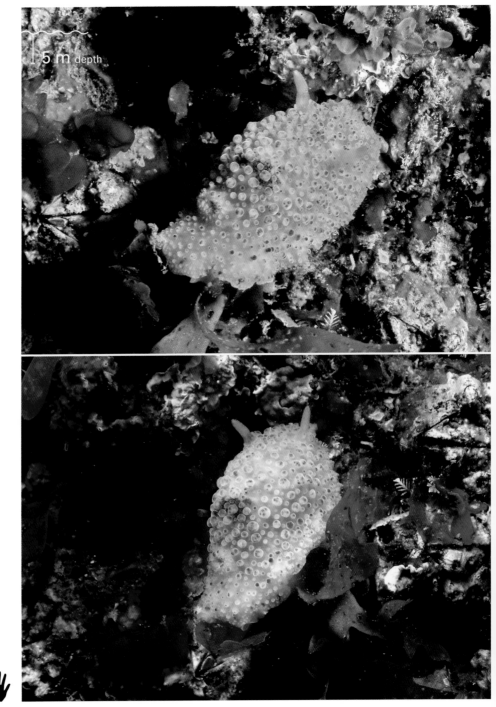

Morphology

Body medium, oval, flat. Color light brown to beige; brown or orange in foot. Dorsum with many rounded tubercles. Mantle skirt covering entire body. Large tubercles on mantle occasionally having stalks. Mouth divided laterally, with oral tentacles on both edges. Rhinophore sheath with a pair of shields. About 4-5 tripinnate gills surrounding anus. Gill sheath surrounded by small tubercles. BL: 50-80 mm long

Remarks

This species lives under rocks or in rock crevices from the lower intertidal zone to a depth of 20 m. In Korea, this species has a variety of morphological variations, but they are all recognized as a single species. More taxonomic research on these variants is required.

Distribution

This is found in Korea, Japan (Honshu), China, and Taiwan and is known as a temperate species based on its distribution. In Korea, it has been observed on the coasts of Jeju Island, the West Sea, the South Sea, the East Sea, Ulleungdo, and Dokdo.

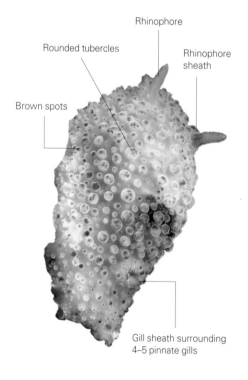

Rhinophore

Rounded tubercles

Rhinophore sheath

Brown spots

Gill sheath surrounding 4–5 pinnate gills

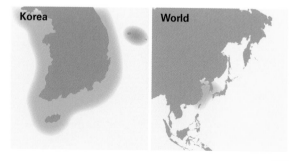

Korea

World

Chromodoris orientalis Rudman, 1983

15 m depth

EN
RA
ES
IV
S

Morphology

Body small to medium, oval, flat. Color white, lined by dark yellow border, with black spots on dorsum. Mantle skirt covering entire body. Posterior tip of foot projecting out. Mouth divided laterally, with oral tentacles on both edges. Rhinophore pinnately compound, with yellow tips that become pale at base. About 12-18 pinnate gills surrounding anus, lined with yellow and black. BL: to 30 mm long

Remarks

This species is one of the most representative sea slugs in Korea. It is commonly found to a depth of 20 m on rocky shores or around adherent invertebrates, especially hydra colonies or in the lower intertidal zone. Mating usually occurs around July to August.

Distribution

This species has a range that includes Korea, Japan (a subregion of Honshu), China, Hong Kong, and Tahiti. In Korea, it can be found on all coasts and, on Dokdo, it occurs everywhere along the coast.

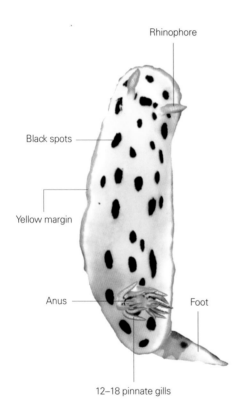

Rhinophore

Black spots

Yellow margin

Anus

Foot

12–18 pinnate gills

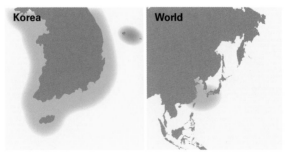

Korea

World

Goniobranchus tinctorius(Rüppell & Leuckart, 1830)

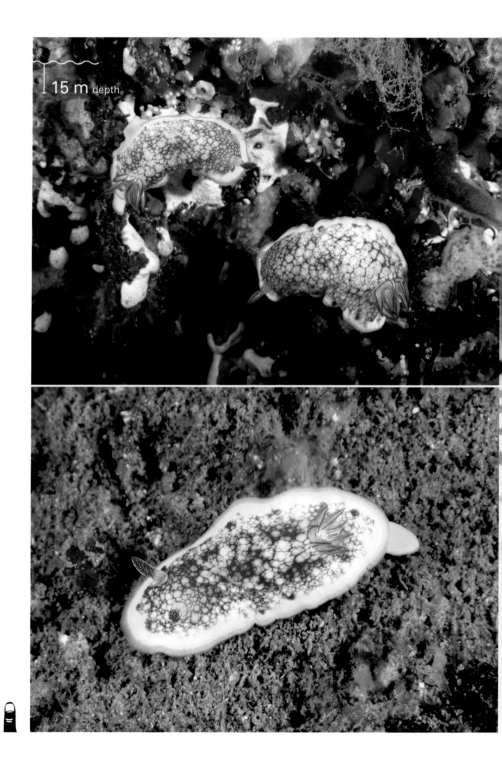

15 m depth

EN
RA
ES
IV
S

Morphology

Body small to medium, oval, flat. Color white, lined by dark yellow border, with red net pattern on dorsum. Mantle skirt covering entire body. Posterior tip of foot projecting out. Mouth divided laterally, with oral tentacles on both edges. Rhinophore pinnately compound, with red tips that become pale at base. About 8-10 pinnate gills surrounding anus, lined with red or orange. BL: to 40 mm long

Remarks

This species lives under rocks or in rock crevices from the lower intertidal zone to a depth of 15 m. In Korea, its scientific name is *Chromodoris tinctoria* (Ruppell & Leuckart), which is a synonym for *Goniobranchus tinctorius*.

Distribution

It is a southern species known to inhabit tropical and subtropical regions in Korea, Japan (Sagami Bay, a subregion of Sado), China, and Taiwan. In Korea, it is mainly found on Jeju Island, in the southern West Sea, on offshore islands in the South Sea, on Ulleungdo, and on Dokdo.

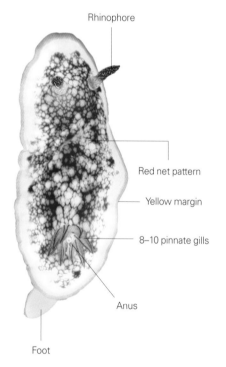

Rhinophore

Red net pattern

Yellow margin

8–10 pinnate gills

Anus

Foot

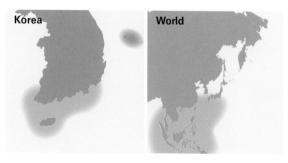

Korea

World

Goniobranchus aureopurpureus
(Collingwood, 1881)

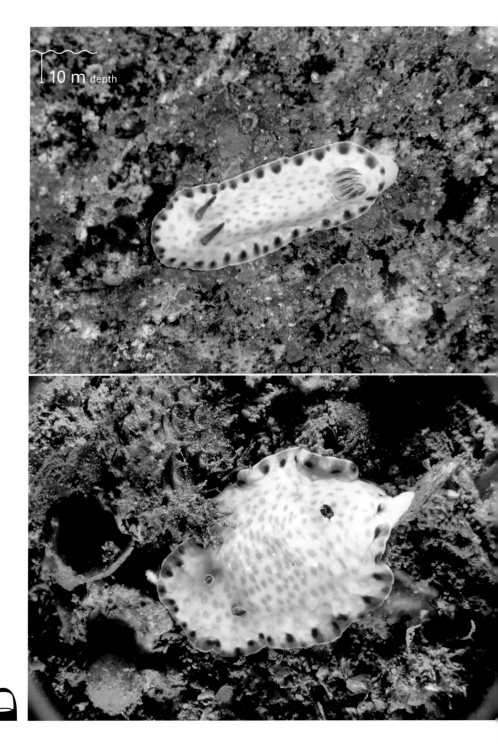

10 m depth

EN
RA
ES
IV
S

Morphology

Body small to medium, oval, flat. Color white, with purple-spotted border. Dorsum with small yellow or brown spots. Mantle skirt covering entire body. Posterior tip of foot projecting out. Mouth divided laterally, with tentacles on both edges. Rhinophore pinnately compound with dark purple tips that become pale at base. About 8-10 pinnate gills surrounding anus, lined with purple. BL: to 40 mm long

Remarks

This species lives under rocks or in rock crevices from the lower intertidal zone to a depth of 15 m and is usually found around sponges. In Korea, its scientific name is *Chromodoris aureopurpurea* Collingwood, which is a synonym for *Goniobranchus aureopurpureus.*

Distribution

It is a southern species known to occur in all tropical and subtropical regions, including southern Korea, a subregion of Hokkaido in Japan, China, and Taiwan. In Korea, it is found on Jeju Island, in the southern West Sea, on offshore islands in the South Sea, on Ulleungdo, and on Dokdo. It has also been observed at Gajebawi Rock and Dongdo on Dokdo.

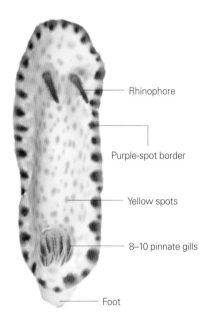

Rhinophore

Purple-spot border

Yellow spots

8–10 pinnate gills

Foot

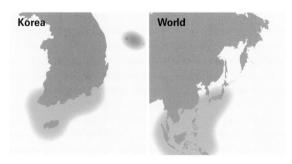

Korea

World

Hypselodoris festiva (A. Adams, 1861)

15 m depth

Morphology

Body small to medium, flat, elongate-oval. Color blue, with intense yellow border. Dorsum with 3 rows of yellow dots or lines. Mantle skirt covering entire body. Posterior tip of foot projecting out like a tail. Mouth divided laterally, with oral tentacles on both edges. Rhinophore pinnately compound with orange tips that become white at base. Twelve white pinnate gills surrounding anus, lined with orange. BL: to 40 mm long

Remarks

This species is one of the most representative sea slugs in Korea. It lives under rocks or in rock crevices from the lower intertidal zone to a depth of 15 m and is commonly found around sponges rich in fiber. Like *C. orientalis*, mating is usually observed around July to August.

Distribution

It is found in Korea, Japan (subregion of Honshu to Kyushu), and China (Bohai and Hong Kong), with the characteristics of a temperate species. In Korea, it can be observed on all coasts and is found all across Dokdo.

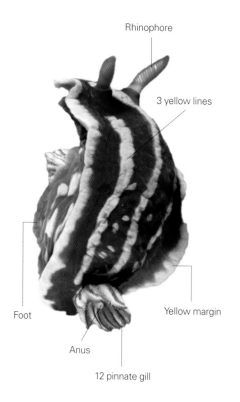

Rhinophore

3 yellow lines

Foot

Yellow margin

Anus

12 pinnate gill

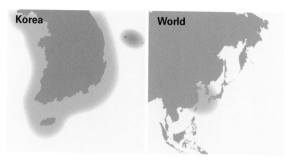

Korea

World

Aldisa cooperi Robilliard & Baba, 1972

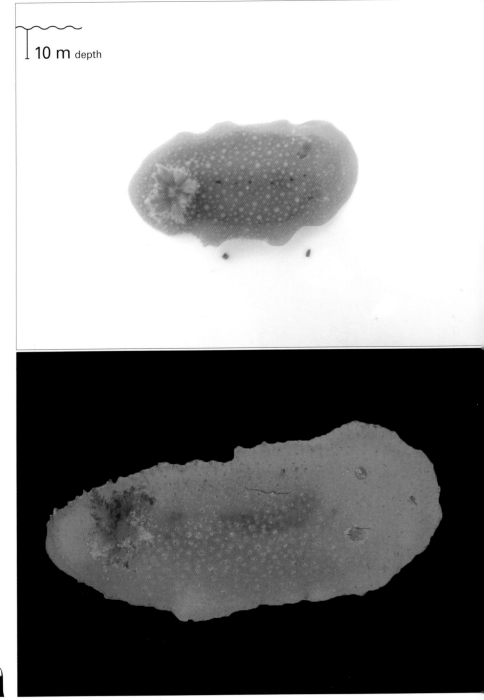

10 m depth

Morphology

Body small, oval, flat. Color yellow or orange. Dorsum densely covered with small projections. A row of black spots running along midline. Mantle skirt covering entire body. Posterior tip of foot projecting out. Mouth divided laterally, with short vestigial tentacles on both edges. Rhinophore multi-layered except for stalk. Base surrounded by small tubercles. Seven gills surrounding anus. Serration-like wrinkles running along edge of gills. BL: to 20 mm long

Remarks

This species lives under rocks or in rock crevices from the lower intertidal zone to a depth of 15 m. This sea slug often lays eggs around reddish sponges in the water.

Distribution

It is found in Korea, Japan, China, Taiwan, and the United States (California to Alaska) and exhibits the characteristics of a northern species by inhabiting seas affected by cold currents. In Korea, it is mainly observed on the coast of the East Sea, on Ulleungdo, and on Dokdo.

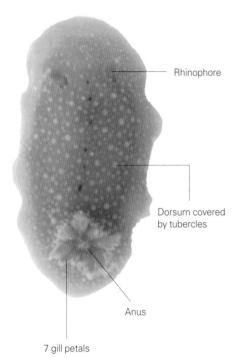

Rhinophore

Dorsum covered by tubercles

Anus

7 gill petals

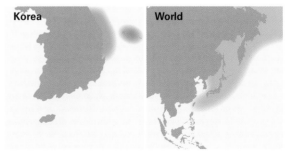

Korea

World

Dendrodoris krusensternii (Gray, 1850)

EN
RA
ES
IV
S

Morphology

Body medium to large, oval, slightly inflated. Color nut brown to brown, with blue fluorescent spots. Dorsum with 2 rows of wrinkled tubercles. Mantle skirt covering entire body. Tubercles arising along margin. Glands arranged outside. Mouth surrounded by tentacles. Rhinophore multi-layered; base surrounded by highly raised tubercles. About 4-5 gills tripinnate surrounding anus, serrated at edge. BL: 70-100 mm long

Remarks

This species lives from the lower intertidal zone to a depth of 30 m in the subtidal zone. It is observed all year round crawling on rocks or invertebrates such as sponges. In Korea, the scientific name for this species is *Dendrodoris denisoni* (Angas), which is a synonym for *Dendrodoris krusensternii*.

Distribution

This species is found in both tropical and temperate regions, including Korea, Japan (Sado Island to a subregion of Sagami Bay), China, Taiwan, Australia, the Indo-West Pacific Coast, and New Caledonia. It is present on all coasts in Korea, though it is most common on Jeju Island, on offshore islands in the West Sea and the South Sea, in the southern East Sea, on Ulleungdo, and on Dokdo.

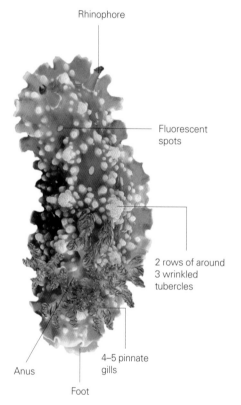

Rhinophore

Fluorescent spots

2 rows of around 3 wrinkled tubercles

4–5 pinnate gills

Anus

Foot

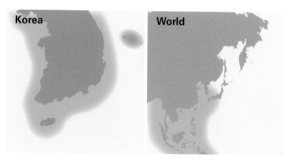

Korea

World

Dermatobranchus otome Baba, 1992

20 m depth

EN
RA
ES
IV
T

Morphology

Body small, elongate. Dorsum with fine longitudinal wrinkles bearing irregular brown zebra patterns with black spots. Rhinophore vertically wrinkled, orange at tip, white at base. Gill arranged horizontally under mantle. Black horizontal bands occasionally present on 1/3 of body. BL: about 10 mm long

Remarks

This species occurs from the lower intertidal zone to depths of 30 m in the subtidal zone. It is particularly common in areas with a high density of anthozoans. This species is often misidentified as *Dermatobranchus striatus* Van Hasselt.

Distribution

According to records, this species has only been found in Korea and Japan (in a subregion of the Boso Peninsula), and they have the characteristics of a temperate species. In Korea, it has been observed on Jeju Island, in the southern West Sea, on offshore islands in the South Sea, on Ulleungdo, and on Dokdo.

Orange rhinophore

Black spots

1 black stripe

Foot

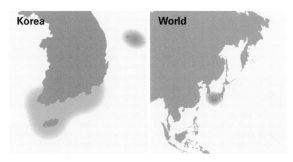

Korea

World

Tritonia festiva (Stearns, 1873)

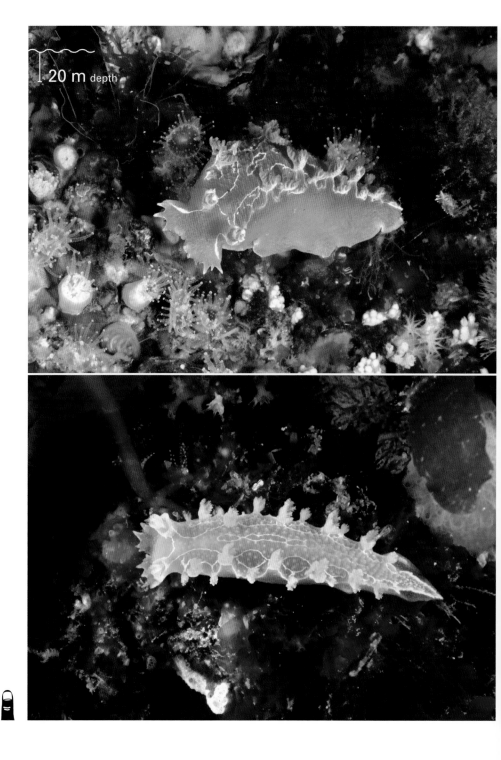

20 m depth

EN
RA
ES
IV
N

Morphology

Body medium to large. Color translucent orange or purple, with white lines on mantle, gills and head shield. Head shield covering mouth, with serrated tip. Rhinophore having a long stalk with club-like pointed tip, surrounded by a serrated sheath. Tubercle-like gills lined up in 2 rows along mantle margin; occasionally 8-9 pairs. Gill tubercle branched. BL: over 80 mm long

Remarks

This species inhabits the lower intertidal zone to a depth of 30 m (or deeper) in the subtidal zone. In Korea, it is commonly observed around anthozoans, including strawberry soft coral.

Distribution

It occurs in Korea, Japan (Hokkaido to Sagami Bay), China, and the United States (the northern coast of California to Alaska) and has the characteristics of a northern species. In Korea, it is mainly observed on the coast of the East Sea, on Ulleungdo, and on Dokdo, and is rarely found on Jeju Island, in the southern West Sea, and on offshore islands in the South Sea.

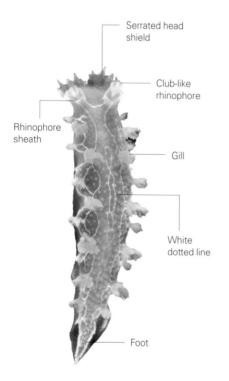

Serrated head shield

Club-like rhinophore

Rhinophore sheath

Gill

White dotted line

Foot

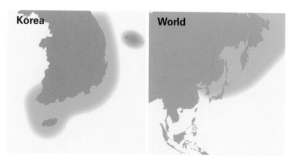

Korea

World

Hermissenda crassicornis (Eschscholtz, 1831)

10 m depth

EN
RA
ES
IV
N

Morphology

Body small to medium. Color translucent white or olive, with an orange middle line surrounded by blueish-white stripes; some individuals with line extending from tentacle to foot. Oral tentacles absent; head tentacle very flexible. Rhinophore erect, with 8-10 wrinkles; some individuals without wrinkles. Gill dark brown, with numerous projections (cerata), arranged in 5-6 pairs along mantle skirt. BL: over 30 mm long

Remarks

This species occurs from the lower intertidal zone to a depth of 30 m (or deeper) in the subtidal zone. It is commonly found around hydra colonies and frequently appears in winter.

Distribution

It is a northern species found in Korea, Japan (Hokkaido to Honshu), China, Taiwan, and North America (Mexico, California, and Alaska). In Korea, it is rarely observed on Jeju Island, in the southern West Sea, and on offshore islands in the South Sea; however, it is quite frequently found in the East Sea, on Ulleungdo, and on Dokdo.

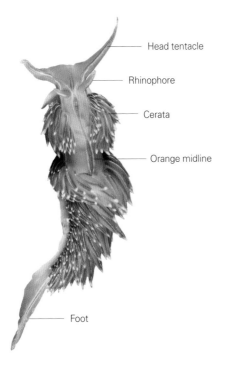

Head tentacle

Rhinophore

Cerata

Orange midline

Foot

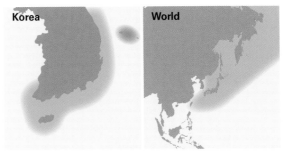

Korea

World

Sakuraeolis japonica (Baba, 1937)

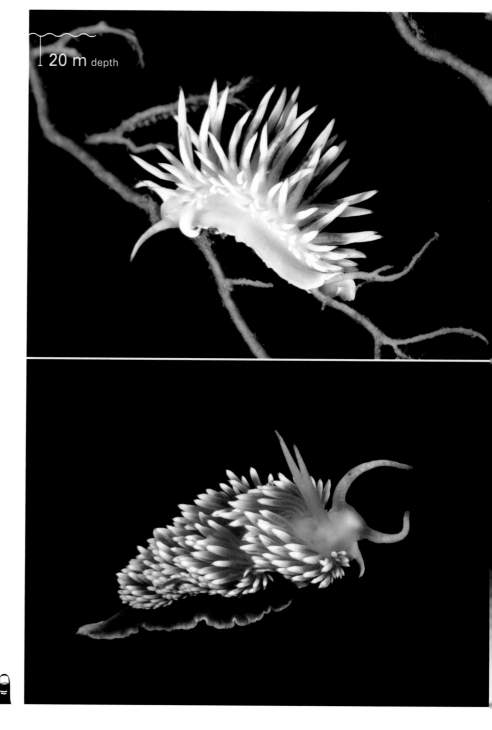

20 m depth

EN
RA
ES
IV
T

Morphology

Body medium. Color white or milky white; occasionally, light pink between head tentacles and rhinophores. Oral tentacles absent, head tentacles very flexible. Rhinophores erect at base, smooth. Gill white, forming numerous cerata, arranged in 7-8 pairs along mantle skirt. Occasionally, apricot-colored stripes appearing in gills due to intestines. Foot arching at anterior end, grooved centrally, pointed at posterior end. BL: 30-50 mm long

Remarks

This species occurs from the lower intertidal zone to a depth of 30 m (or deeper) in the subtidal zone. In Korea, it feeds on and lays eggs around *Solanderia misakinensis*. The scientific name of this species in Korea is *Sakuraeolis modesta* (Bergh), which is a synonym for *Sakuraeolis japonica*. Hirano (1990) divided *Sakuraelis japonica* into *Sakuraelis gerberina* and *Sakuraelis sakuracea* and reported them as new species, but the specimens collected in Korea have characteristics of both.

Distribution

This species is known to be found only in Korea and Japan and exhibits the characteristics of a temperate species. In Korea, it is rarely observed on Jeju Island, in the southern West Sea, and on offshore islands in the South Sea; however, it is quite frequently found in the East Sea, on Ulleungdo, and on Dokdo.

Head tentacles

Rhinophore

Gill cerata

Foot

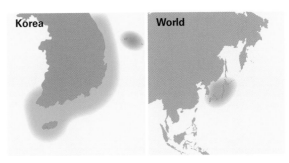

Korea

World

Protaeolidiella atra Baba, 1955

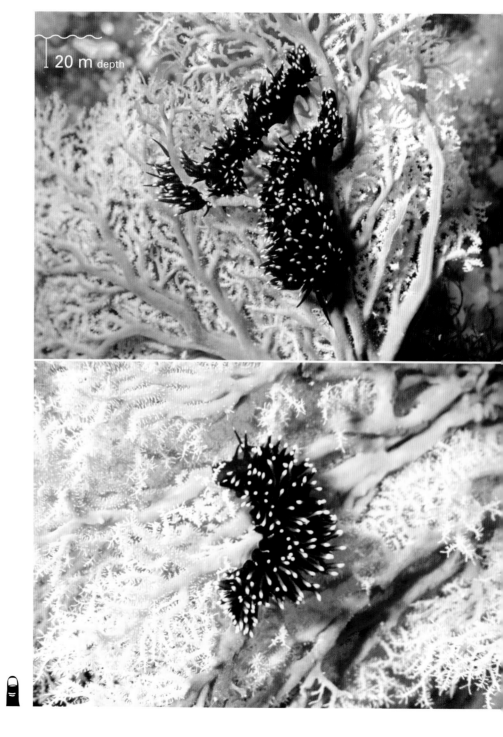

20 m depth

Morphology

Body small to medium. Color blackish except for foot. Head tentacles and cerata flexible, white at tips. Mouth grooved up and down, without oral tentacles. Rhinophore located on dorsum, with erect and smooth base. Gills forming numerous cerata, arranged in 1-3 pairs along mantle skirt. BL: over 30 mm long

Remarks

This species occurs from the lower intertidal zone to a depth of 30 m (or deeper) in the subtidal zone. In Korea, it feeds on the polyps of *Solanderia misakinensis* and lays pink eggs on its branches. *Protaeolidiella juliae* (Burn) is the same species.

Distribution

This species is found in Korea, Japan (Honshu), China, Taiwan, Australia, Papua New Guinea, New Caledonia, and Tanzania and has the characteristics of a southern species. In Korea, it is not commonly found, but it is observed on Jeju Island, in the southern West Sea, on offshore islands in the South Sea, in the East Sea, on Ulleungdo, and on Dokdo.

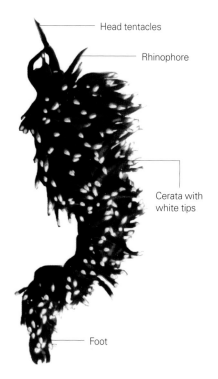

Head tentacles

Rhinophore

Cerata with white tips

Foot

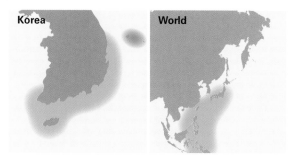

Korea

World

Siphonaria sirius Pilsbry, 1894

Intertidal
zone

EN
RA
ES
IV
T

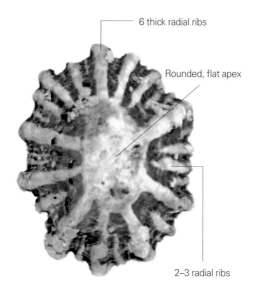

6 thick radial ribs

Rounded, flat apex

2–3 radial ribs

Morphology

Shell lowly conical, oval in underside. Apex situated anteriorly, mostly eroded in mature individuals. Color black. About 5-6 white radial ribs strongly projected with secondary ribs among them. Inside of apex milky-white, surrounded by yellowish-white zone. Adductor scar located at internal center. Siphonal canal opening toward the right. BL: about 15 mm long

Remarks

It lives mainly around barnacle colonies in the middle of the rocky intertidal zone, in tidepools, or on rocks with low-lying pools. In Korea, two species of Siphonariidae have been recorded: *Siphonaria sirius* Pilsbry and *Siphonaria japonica*. They breathe with an air sac (or lung sac) because they do not have gills.

Distribution

This species is known to inhabit tropical and temperate regions such as Korea, Japan (Honshu to Kyushu), China, and Taiwan. In Korea, it is found on Jeju Island, in the southern West Sea (Gageodo), on offshore islands in the South Sea, in the southern East Sea, on Ulleungdo, and on Dokdo.

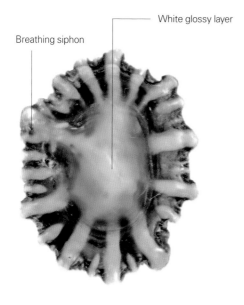

White glossy layer

Breathing siphon

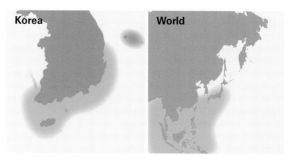

Korea

World

Siphonaria japonica (Donovan, 1824)

Intertidal zone

Morphology

Shell small, thin, conical, ovate in underside. Apex situated posteriorly, slightly curved, eroded in mature individuals. Color dark brown. Around 24 light-brown radial ribs clearly projected. Inside of apex milky white, surrounded by yellowish-white zone. C-shaped adductor scar located at internal center. BL: about 15 mm long

Remarks

It lives mainly around barnacle colonies in the middle of the rocky intertidal zone or adheres to wet rocks. Large populations may exist in some regions while it is not found at all in others, but it is more common than *Siphonaria sirius*. Together with land snails, these two species belong to the *Pulmonata* family, which has changed significantly in the traditional classification system. As such, this species is still treated as an informal group. In Korea, it is classified as a subfamily.

Distribution

It is known to inhabit tropical and temperate regions such as Korea, Japan, China, and Hong Kong, and it is found on all Korean coasts. In Dokdo, it has been found behind Dongdo wharf, opposite Seodo wharf, and on Gajebawi Rock.

Fine, dense radial ribs

Pointed, curved apex

Thin, weak margin

Respiratory canal

Black glossy layer

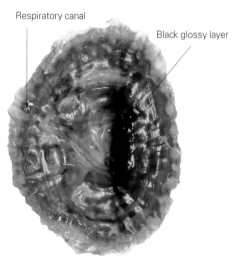

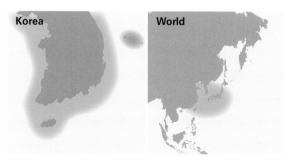

Korea

World

Invertebrates of Dokdo Island Mollusks

Class Bivalvia

The class Bivalvia obtains its name from the two valves (i.e., shells) of its member species. The class was previously named Pelecypoda (Gr. *pelekus* ["hatchet"] + *pous*, *podus*) because their foot looks like a hand ax when it emerges from the shell. This class appeared during the Ordovician period. More than 25,000 species are known worldwide, with 490 found in Korea.

The most recognizable characteristic of bivalves is their two shells. The side with the siphonal canal is the posterior end, while the side with the foot is the anterior end. The visceral mass is attached to the midline of the dorsum. The gills are thin and wide on both sides, and the movement of the cilia in the gills causes the water to flow for feeding. Species in this class do not have a head or radula. Most live in the sand or mud, but some adhere firmly to the bedrock with a byssus or calcareous structure or create a hole to sit in. When a scallop swims, it claps its valves together to "bounce" through the water.

Arca boucardi Jousseaume, 1894

20 m depth

EN

RA

ES

IV

T

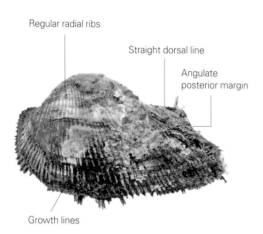

Regular radial ribs

Straight dorsal line

Angulate
posterior margin

Growth lines

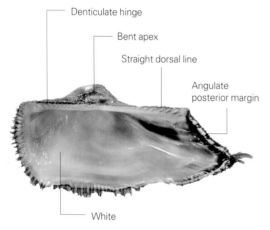

Denticulate hinge

Bent apex

Straight dorsal line

Angulate
posterior margin

White

Morphology

Shell almost rectangular. Umbo located anteriorly. Periostracum light brown, bearing regular radial ribs. Brown hairs present on ventral or posterior margins or between radial ribs. Hinge margin obliquely denticulate; dorsal margin straight; posterior margin angulate. Inside of shell white, brown, with anterior and posterior adductor scars, pallial sinus absent. BL: about 50 mm long

Remarks

This species uses its byssal thread to adhere to rocks from the lower intertidal zone to a depth of 50 m. Depending on habitat, morphological variation diverse. On Ulleungdo or Dokdo, it forms large colonies with oysters on sheer rocky cliffs. Its Korean name can be translated as "rectangular seashell."

Distribution

This is a temperate species found in Korea, Russia (Vladivostok), Japan (South Hokkaido to Okinawa), China, and Taiwan. In Korea, it is commonly found on Jeju Island and below Anmyeondo in the West Sea, in the South Sea, in the East Sea, on Ulleungdo, and on Dokdo. On Dokdo, it is commonly seen on Gajebawi Rock, and has also been observed on the outskirts of Seodo.

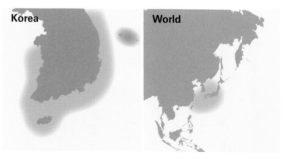

Korea

World

Porterius dalli (E. A. Smith, 1885)

EN
RA
ES
IV
T

Morphology

Shell small to medium, elongate-elliptical; anterior end low; posterior end high. Umbo situated at anterior end. Periostracum crossing growth ribs, forming lattice pattern. Inside of shell white. Teeth horizontal, parallel to dorsal margin. BL: about 35 mm long

Remarks

This species usually lives under large rocks or rock formations from the lower intertidal zone to a depth of 50 m. Usually, 3-4 seashells are attached to a single rock using their byssal threads. This species is a member of the family *Parallelodontidae*, and only this species has been reported.

Distribution

This is a temperate species found in Korea, in Japan (southern Hokkaido to the Seto Inland Sea), and on the coast of the Yellow Sea in China. In Korea, it has been recorded on Jeju Island, in the southern West Sea (Uido), in the South Sea, in the East Sea, on Ulleungdo, and on Dokdo, but has not been observed in the northwestern region of the West Sea. In Dokdo, it is found across the south side of Dongdo wharf and around Gajebawi Rock.

Apex curved forward

Growth lines

Regular radial ribs

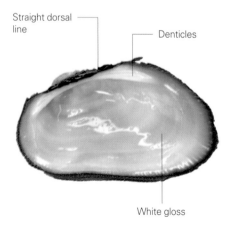

Straight dorsal line

Denticles

White gloss

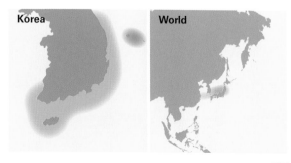

Korea

World

Mytilus coruscus Gould, 1861

15 m depth

Morphology

Shell large, elongate-ovate, with narrow anterior end. Periostracum very thick, blackish, glossy; umbonal area purplish. Inside of shell milky-white, nacreous, occasionally tinted with blue. Umbo situated at anterior end, curved. Ventral margin almost straight. Dorsal margin angulate in middle, parallel to ventral margin. BL: about 150 mm long

Remarks

This seashell attaches rigidly to the surface of large rocks with its byssal thread from the lower intertidal zone to a depth of 50 m. It usually forms large colonies at a depth of 5-15 m and is a well-known fishery resource. It is hermaphrodite, with the female flesh colored red and the male flesh apricot or ivory. On Ulleungdo, mussel rice is sold as a local dish.

Distribution

This species is found in Korea, Japan (Hokkaido to Kyushu), China, and the temperate and subpolar regions of Alaska. In Korea, it is found from Jeju Island to the northern East Coast (Goseong). The mussels at Ulleungdo and Dokdo are the largest and have the highest density. In the West Sea (Baekryeongdo) and the South Sea, it is mainly found on offshore islands.

Moderately curved posterior-dorsal margin

Bent umbo

Thick shell

No umbilicus

Milky-white, intensely nacreous interior

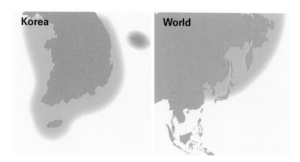

Korea

World

Leiosolenus lischkei Huber, 2010

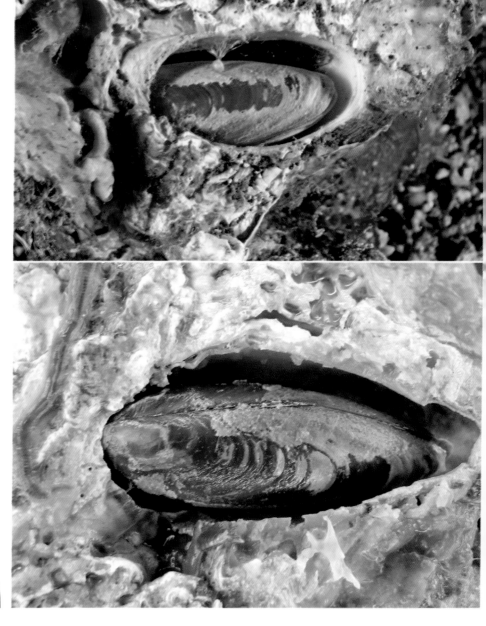

Morphology

Shell small, cylindrical, smooth, brittle, with elongate-ovate contour. Color brownish. Umbo situated at higher anterior end. Ventral margin slightly inflated, straight; dorsal margin weakly angulate at ligament. Inside of shell nacreous. Mantle having a gland releasing acid that dissolves calcareous structures to create holes that are used to attach the byssal thread to rock. BL: about 35 mm long

Remarks

This species makes holes in limestone or oyster shells from the lower intertidal zone to a depth of around 40 m. It occasionally lives on the thick shell of sea snails. In Korea, its scientific name is *Lithophaga curta* (Lischke), which recently became a synonym for *Leiosolenus lischkei*.

Distribution

It is known to live in temperate regions such as Korea, Japan (Honshu to Kyushu), China (East China Sea), and Taiwan. It has not been found in the northern West Sea or the northern East Sea in Korea. It occurs on Jeju Island, in the southern West Sea (Gageodo), in the South Sea, in the East Sea (Samchuck), on Ulleungdo, and on Dokdo.

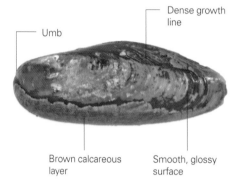

Umb

Dense growth line

Brown calcareous layer

Smooth, glossy surface

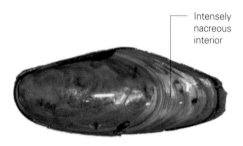

Intensely nacreous interior

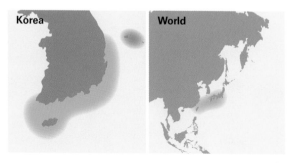

Korea

World

Modiolus modiolus (Linnaeus, 1758)

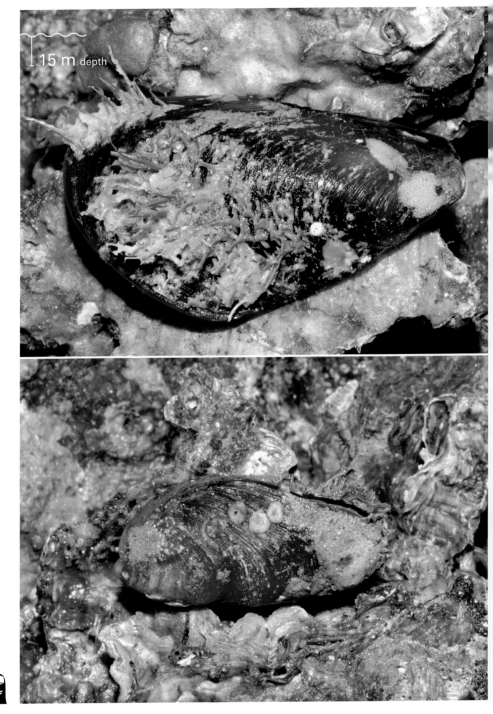

15 m depth

EN

RA

ES

IV

N

Morphology

Shell medium to large, thin, brown in color. Umbo inflated, situated on antero-dorsal side. Periostracum black. Anterior margin with bristles; ventral margin straight, slightly convex; byssal retractor hole relatively wide. Inside of shell reddish-purple on dorsal side, milky white, nacreous on ventral side. BL: about 70 mm long (specimen in the east coast of Korea generally larger)

Remarks

This seashell is commonly observed around the substrates of brown algae, large sea squirts, or oysters from the lower intertidal zone to a depth of 50 m. It is often found in polluted areas, such as on the walls of ports. In Korea, its scientific name is *Modiolus kurilensis* (Bernard), which was recently recognized as a synonym for *Modiolus modiolus*.

Distribution

It is known as a northern species that is found from Jeju Island in Korea to above Tokyo Bay in Japan and Russia. In Korea, it has been recorded on Jeju Island, in the central West Sea (Taean), in the South Sea, and in the East Sea (Goseong). This geographical distribution indicates that the central East Sea is its southern limit. In Dokdo, it is found around Dongdo wharf and Gajebawi Rock.

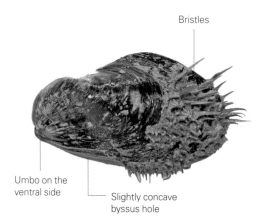

Bristles

Umbo on the ventral side

Slightly concave byssus hole

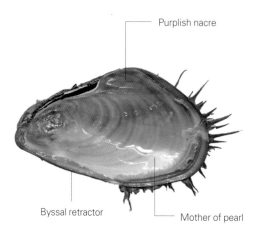

Purplish nacre

Byssal retractor

Mother of pearl

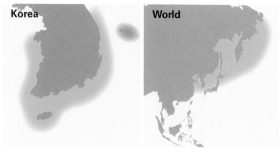

Korea

World

Modiolus nipponicus (Oyama, 1950)

10 m depth

EN
RA
ES
IV
T

Morphology

Shell small, thin, inflated. Umbo blunt, located at anterior end of dorsum. Color reddish-brown, covered with yellowish-brown periostracum. Surface with yellowish-brown bristles except for umbo and antero-ventral margin. Ventral margin straight, slightly dented; byssal hole slightly wide. Inside of shell blackish-purple at umbonal area, bluish-green at dorsum, white, nacreous at middle. BL: about 30 mm long

Remarks

This seashell is commonly observed around the substrates of brown algae, large sea squirts, or oysters from the lower intertidal zone to a depth of 50 m. Its morphology is similar to *Modiolus modiolus* and *Modiolus auriculatus*, but its shell profile is different.

Distribution

It is known to be widely distributed across temperate regions such as Korea and Japan (Honshu to Kyushu). It is found on all coasts of Korea. In Dokdo, it is commonly found on Dongdo and Seodo and Gajebawi Rock.

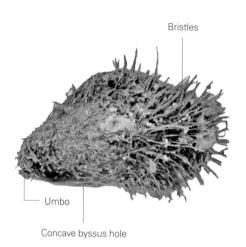

Bristles

Umbo

Concave byssus hole

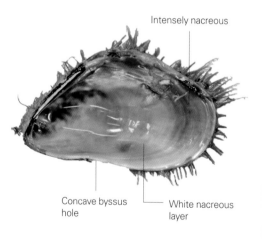

Intensely nacreous

Concave byssus hole

White nacreous layer

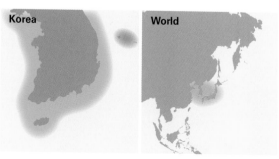

Korea

World

Septifer keenae Nomura, 1936

5 m depth

EN
RA
ES
IV
T

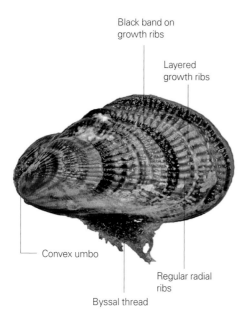

Black band on
growth ribs

Layered
growth ribs

Convex umbo

Regular radial
ribs

Byssal thread

Morphology

Shell small to medium, thin, inflated, covered with dark-brown periostracum. Umbo situated anteriorly. Radial ribs extending regularly from umbo, crossed by growth ribs. Growth ribs occasionally thick, nut brown to black. Ventral margin straight, slightly dented. Posterior margin round, parallel to ventral margin. Inside of shell white, nacreous. BL: about 30 mm long

Remarks

This species is less common than *Septifer virgatus*. It is sometimes confused with that species but can be easily distinguished by the comb-like radial ribs on its shell. However, *Septifer virgatus* individuals with an unclear or flattened comb pattern can be confused with *Septifer keenae* Noruma. In Korea, all four species in this genus have been recorded. *Septifer biocularis* was once reported in Dokdo, but it is not yet clear if it lives there or not. This is because the comb pattern on its shell is similar to *Septifer keenae* Noruma.

Distribution

It is considered to be a temperate species found mainly in Korea and Japan (southern Hokkaido to Kyushu). In Korea, it has not been recorded in the northern West Sea or in the northern East Sea. On Dokdo, it is found near the surface of the intertidal zone on Seodo and Dongdo.

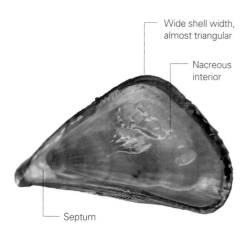

Wide shell width,
almost triangular

Nacreous
interior

Septum

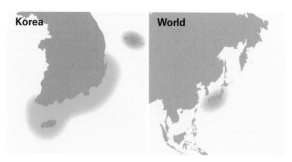

Korea

World

Septifer virgatus (Wiegmann, 1837)

Intertidal zone

EN
RA
ES
IV
T

Morphology

Shell solid, elongate-ovate. Umbo pointed, located on left side, bearing weak radial ribs with clear growth striae. Color mainly reddish-purple at middle, black at postero-dorsal line. Ventral margin slightly concave, almost parallel to postero-dorsal end. Posterior margin large, round. Inside of shell reddish-purple, with septum around umbo. BL: about 40 mm long

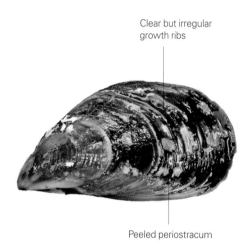

Clear but irregular growth ribs

Peeled periostracum

Remarks

This species is attached to rocks in the middle or lower intertidal zone, often forming large colonies in areas affected by waves. It serves as important habitat for invertebrates in the intertidal zone along with barnacles. Because juveniles have strong radial ribs that mostly fade as they mature, this species is often mistaken by the shape of the shell. This species has a small septum located in the interior around the umbones area, which is the largest feature of *Septifer* species.

Distribution

This is a temperate species found in Korea, Japan (Hokkaido to Kyushu), China (East China Sea to Hong Kong), Taiwan, and Australia. It occurs all over Korea. It is also found over the entire coast of Dokdo and forms large colonies near the water surface.

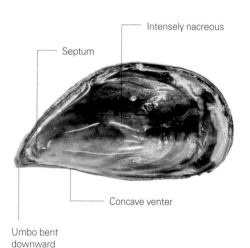

Intensely nacreous

Septum

Concave venter

Umbo bent downward

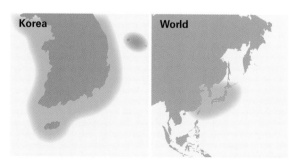

Korea

World

Laevichlamys cuneata (Reeve, 1853)

20 m depth

Morphology

Shell small, thin, ovate. Color yellow, red to brown, with irregularly arranged patterns. Valve equally inflated. Right valve with weak radial ribs occasionally crossed by concentric lines. Left valve with radial ribs of 5-6 strong scale-like tubercles. BL: about 30 mm long

Remarks

This species lives in rock crevices or adheres to the bottom of rocks from the lower intertidal zone to a depth of 30 m in the subtidal zone. Though it is frequently observed, its population is not large. This species was recently promoted to *Laevichlamys* (Waller, 1993), which has been used as one of the subgenus names for *Chlamys*. Its Korean name, "scallop with unequal ears," originates from the fact that one of its auricles on the large wedge of the umbo is not developed; this feature is observed in many scallops.

Distribution

This is a southern species widely distributed in tropical and subtropical regions, including Korea, Japan (below the Boso Peninsula), China, Taiwan, the Philippines, the United States (Hawaii), and Indonesia. It is found on all coasts of Korea and is widely distributed on Dongdo and Seodo and Gajebawi Rock on Dokdo.

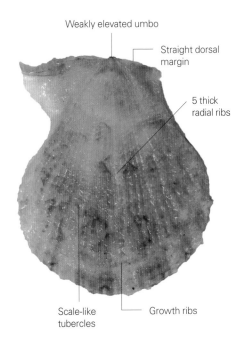

Weakly elevated umbo

Straight dorsal margin

5 thick radial ribs

Scale-like tubercles

Growth ribs

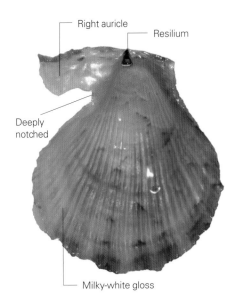

Right auricle

Resilium

Deeply notched

Milky-white gloss

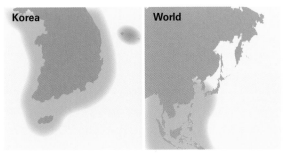

Korea

World

Spondylus squamosus Schreibers, 1793

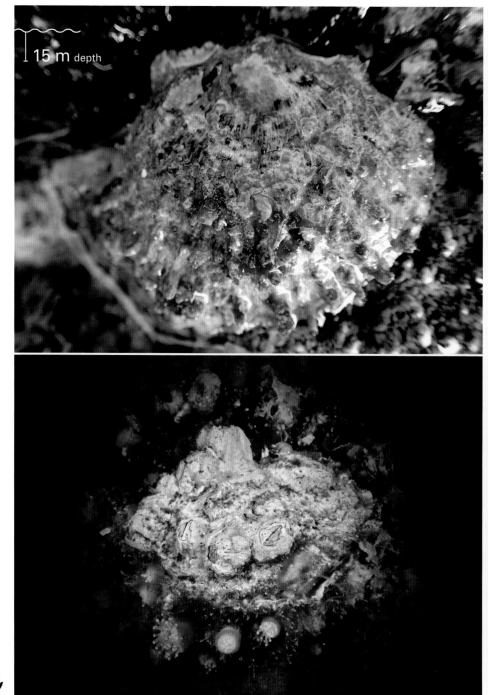

15 m depth

EN
RA
ES
IV
S

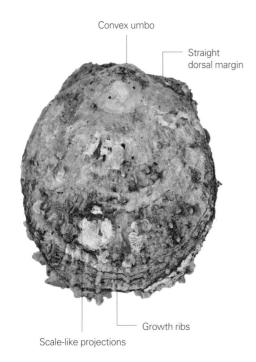

Convex umbo

Straight
dorsal margin

Growth ribs

Scale-like projections

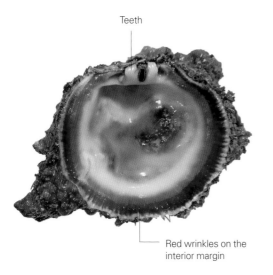

Teeth

Red wrinkles on the
interior margin

Morphology

Shell thick, broad, oval to circular. Valve inflated to a rounded shape. Shell cemented to substrate on its right umbo. Left valve broad, brown to red, with irregular and radially-arranged projections. Projections white, occasionally broken or covered by other fouling organisms, with a spatulate tip. Auricles small, equisized. BL: about 60 mm long

Remarks

This species adheres to rocks from the lower intertidal zone to a depth of 30 m in the subtidal zone. It is usually not visible because it attaches to other oysters or rock crevices. *Spondylus barbatus* Reeve and *Spondylus cruentus* Lischke, which have been used as scientific names for this species, are synonimized.

Distribution

It is known to inhabit tropical and subtropical regions, including Korea, Japan (below the Boso Peninsula to Okinawa), China (Hong Kong), and Taiwan. In Korea, it is mainly found on Jeju Island, in the southern West Sea (Gageodo), in the South Sea, on the coast of the East Sea (Joomunjin), on Ulleungdo, and on Dokdo. On Dokdo, it has been found on Gajebawi Rock and on the annexed islands around Seodo.

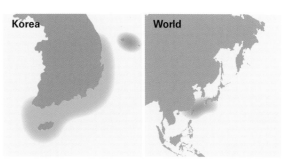

Korea

World

203

Limaria hirasei (Pilsbry, 1901)

Morphology

Shell small, elongate-ovate, thin, flat. Color translucent. Resilium very narrow; anterior auricle gaping wide. Anterior margin straight. Posterior margin round, slightly curved. Lower margin semi-circular. Fine radial ribs densely arranged on surface. When alive, red tentacles extending beyond shell. BL: about 27 mm long

Remarks

This species is known to inhabit rocky areas with sandy substrates from the lower intertidal zone to a depth of 50 m in the subtidal zone. It is usually found under rocks or stones and sometimes on rocks. If this scallop is exposed to danger, it moves its valves to propel itself through the water.

Distribution

It is known to be a temperate species found in Korea, Japan (the Boso Peninsula to Okinawa), China (Hong Kong), and Taiwan. It is found on all coasts of Korea and is most commonly observed on offshore islands. It lives in most coastal areas around Dokdo.

Small, weak umbo

Glossy, translucent surface

Dense radial ribs

Straight dorsal margin

White, translucent interior

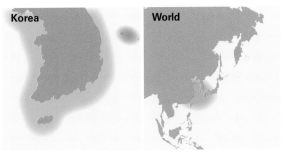

Korea

World

Neopycnodonte cochlear (Poli, 1795)

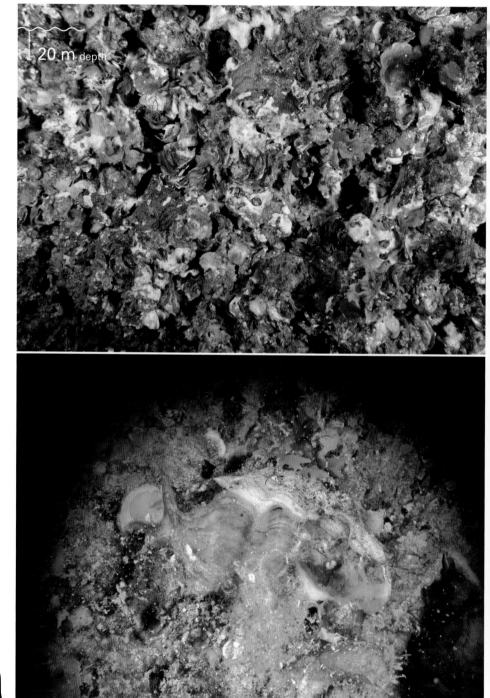

20 m depth

EN

RA

ES

IV

S

Morphology

Shell small, sharp, various in shape depending on substrate. Shell cemented to substrate on its umbo; left valve somewhat inflated; right valve flat or dented. Inside of shell white or light brown. Hinge on left valve wide, thinly spread. BL: about 40 mm long

Remarks

This species lives on rocky shores in the 20-500 m subtidal zone. On Dokdo, they live in clusters on inclined rocks in 20 m deep water, particularly on annexed islands around Seodo or Gajebawi Rock. On Ulleungdo, it is closely attached to cliffs at a depth of 30-50 m, forming large colonies. This species is ecologically important as it acts as the habitat for small fish, crustaceans, and lugworms.

Distribution

This is a southern species known to occur in tropical and subtropical regions such as Korea, Japan, the United States (Hawaii), Chile (Easter Island), and the East African coast. In Korea, it is found on Jeju Island, in the West Sea, in the South Sea, on Ulleungdo and on Dokdo, and is most commonly found on Ulleungdo and Dokdo. It lives all over Dokdo including on Dongdo and Seodo and annexed islands.

Multi-layered right valve

Raised edge of right valve

Thin and sharp attached side on left valve

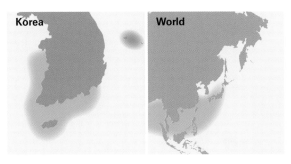

Korea

World

Striostrea circumpicta (Pilsbry, 1904)

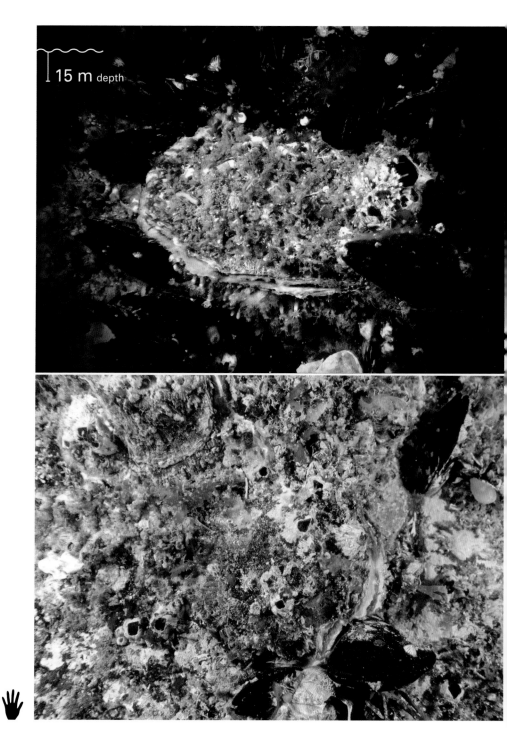

15 m depth

EN
RA
ES
IV
T

Morphology

Shell medium, irregular from rhombus, rectangle, disc or triangle depending on substrate. Right valve less inflated, flat, somewhat concave. Interior margin purplish or dark brown. Lamellae layered on surface. Both sides of ligament lined by tubercles forming wrinkles. BL: about 60 mm long

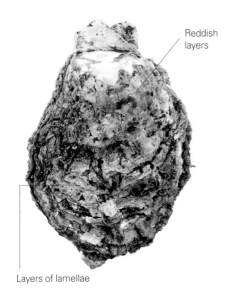

Reddish layers

Layers of lamellae

Remarks

It adheres to rocks from the lower intertidal zone to 30m depth. It is usually clustered, but in some cases, several individuals are scattered. This species is viviparous, which does not spawn its larvae from fertilized eggs but bears them within the shell and releases when they develop into spat (infant oysters). Its Korea name 'Taengsaenggul (Viviparous oyster)' is derived from these developmental characteristics.

Distribution

It occurs in subtropical and temperate regions such as Korea, Japan (Honshu-Kyushu), China (Yellow Sea Coast-East China Sea), and Taiwan. In Korea, it is distributed to Jeju Island, the southern West Sea, offshore islands in the South Sea, the southern East Sea, Ulleungdo and Dokdo. It lives in all parts of Dokdo, being found mainly on Gajebawi Rock.

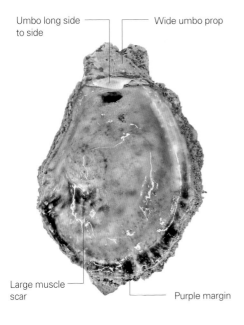

Umbo long side to side

Wide umbo prop

Large muscle scar

Purple margin

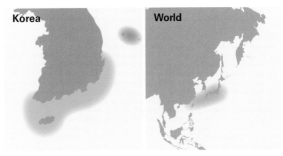

Korea

World

Crassostrea gigas (Thunberg, 1793)

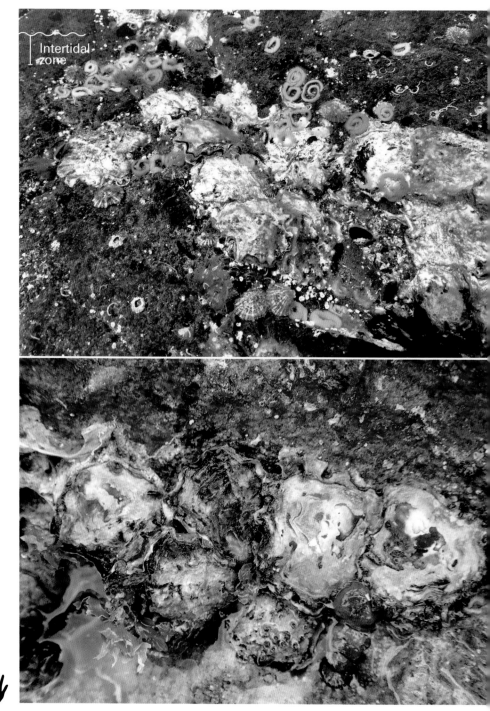

Intertidal zone

EN
RA
ES
IV
T

Morphology

Shell large, variable in shape depending on environment (hemispherical, conical to branch). Left valve very thick. Right valve slightly convex, with layered lamellae forming growth ribs. Margin occasionally wrinkled. BL: over 50 mm long

Remarks

This oyster attaches usually its left valve to rocks or bedrocks from the middle intertidal to the upper subtidal zones. It usually forms large and small communities even in the natural state. Being a very useful marine resource, it is a representative cultured species and one of the most used mollusks worldwide. It well adapts to the changes in water temperature, and is known as a foreign or invasive species in some regions such as the United States and New Zealand.

Distribution

It is a temperate species and naturally distributed in Korea, Japan, China, and Taiwan. In Korea, except for the east coast, oyster farming is done nationwide, which is dominant in the west and south coasts. In Dokdo, it was observed at Gajebawi Rock and the intertidal zone at the Dongdo wharf.

Umbo

Left valve attached to bottom

Low, flat right valve

Wrinkles on margin

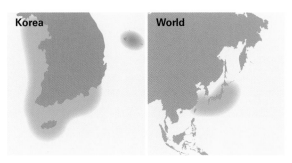

Korea

World

211

Crassostrea nippona (Seki, 1934)

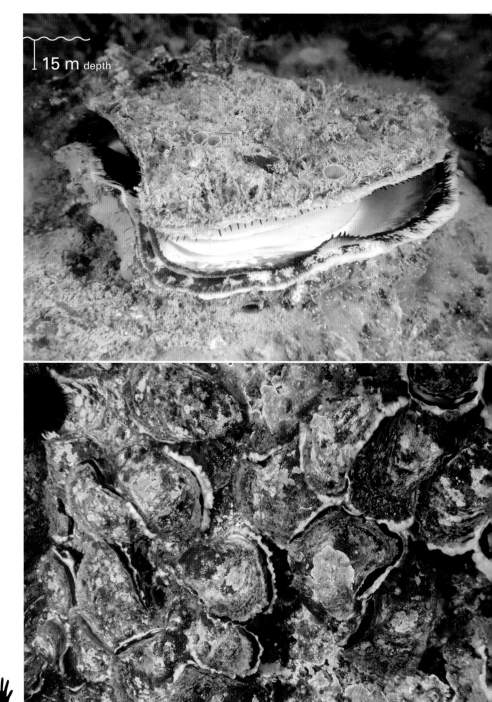

15 m depth

Morphology

Shell large, thick, elongate-oval, wider downward. Anterior and posterior edges somewhat convex. Right valve smaller than left valve. Left valve attached to rocks. Right valve with layered lamellae. Shell of adults bent toward left. Inside of shell white, porcelaneous. BL: to 100 mm long

Remarks

It is distributed in about 30 m deep subtidal zone. It often individually inhabits or forms a clusters of many individuals. It is also eaten and tastes good. It is difficult to collect large amount of this oyster because it is firmly attached to the rock surface. Generally, oysters are difficult to distinguish in water, but this species has a relatively smooth and constant margins when it opens its shell.

Distribution

It is a temperate species distributed from Korea, Japan (Honshu-Kyushu) to China (Yellow Sea). It occurs across the coast in Korea, and is mainly found in the offshore islands of South Sea, Ulleungdo and Dokdo. In Dokdo, it was confirmed in Gajebawi Rock, and it is also found in Dongdo and Seodo.

Vestigial umbo

Thin, sharp periostracum

Densely layered growth ribs

White, porcelaneous interior

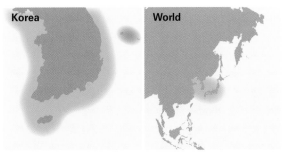

Korea

World

Anomia chinensis Philippi, 1849

10 m depth

Morphology

Shell medium, flat, almost circular, irregular in shape depending on substrate. Left valve inflated, thick, with weak radial ribs. Right valve thin, brittle. Byssus hole located under umbo. Muscle scar reflecting underneath. BL: about 55 mm long

Remarks

It lives in rocky shores from the lower intertidal zone to 10 m deep subtidal zone. In Korea, all three species are known in the family Anomiidae, which are *A. chinensis*, *Monia umbonata*, and *Monia macroschisma*.

Distribution

It is a southern species distributed in Korea, Japan (South Hokkaido-Ryukyu Islands), China (Yellow Sea-Hong Kong), Taiwan, and Indonesia. It is observed all over the coast of Korea, and is commonly found around Dongdo wharf.

Small umbo

Byssus

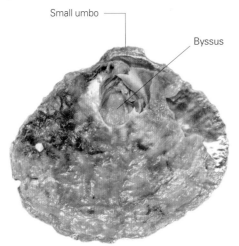

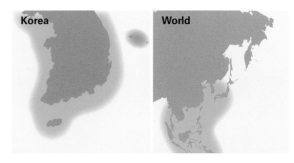

Korea

World

Chama japonica Lamarck, 1819

EN
RA
ES
IV
S

Left valve covering the umbo

Spines on radial ribs

Morphology
Shell small, thick, round. Color usually red. Left valve attached to substrate (rock surface or oyster shell). Right valve low, flat. Spines densely raised along growth ribs. Inside of shell white, glossy, wrinkled along edge. BL: about 20 mm long

Remarks
It is found in 10-50 m depth, and is usually attached to rocks and other oysters. The left valv is larger than the right one. Chama species belongs to Order Veneroida. Its Korea name 'Ajabi Oyster' is made because it lives with oysters even though it is not an oyster.

Distribution
In Korea, it lives in Jeju Island, the southern East Sea, the South Sea, the southern East Sea, Ulleungdo, and Dokdo and appears mainly in areas where S. *circumpicta* occurs. In Dokdo, it is also usually attached to the shell of *S. cirsumpicta*. It is a southern species distributed in Korea, Japan (South Hokkaido-Ryukyu Islands), Southeast Asia, and the Indian Ocean.

Teeth on hinge

Umbo

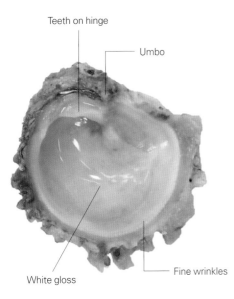

White gloss

Fine wrinkles

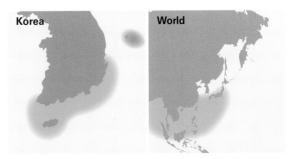

Korea

World

Kellia porculus Pilsbry, 1904

EN
RA
ES
IV
T

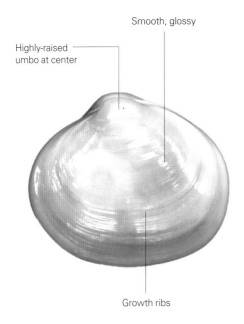

Smooth, glossy

Highly-raised
umbo at center

Growth ribs

Morphology

Shell small, triangular, almost orbicular, equivalve. Color yellowish white, glossy. Umbo rising highly in middle. Growth ribs thin, regular, with about 2 clear rims at bottom. Inside of shell white, glossy. Hinge with teeth. BL: about 10 mm long

Remarks

It lives up to 30 m deep subtidal zone, sometimes being found in the lower indtertidal zone. It is usually found under stones in sandy areas. Compared to other *Kellia* species, this species has two distinct rims in the lower part of the shell.

Distribution

It is known as a temperate species occurring mainly in Korea and Japan (Boso Peninsula-Kyushu). It is distributed on all coasts of Korea, and is mostly found in the southern Dongdo, Seodo and Gajebawi Rock in Dokdo where sandy shores have developed.

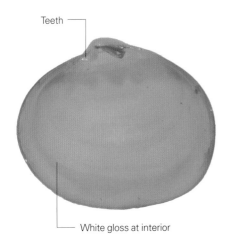

Teeth

White gloss at interior

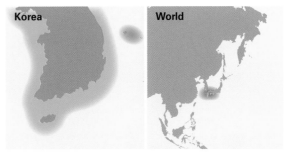

Korea

World

Cardita leana Dunker, 1860

20 m depth

EN
RA
ES
IV
T

Morphology

Shell small, rectangular. Color reddish-brown at anterior side, yellowish-white at posterior side. Umbo situated at left end. Anterior margin straight. Ventral margin slightly concave with byssus hole. Dorsal margin diagonally leading to posterior margin. Surface with 14-18 thick and deep radial ribs of spines present. Inside of shell white to dark-brown. BL: 15-30 mm long

Remarks

It lives the lower intertidal zone to 30 m deep subtidal zone. Mainly, it adheres to holdfasts of large brown algae such as sweet laver or to the bottom of stone.

Distribution

It is known as a temperate species occurring mainly in Korea and Japan (Boso Peninsula-Kyushu). It is distributed on all coasts of Korea, but more common in the offshore island. In Dokdo, it is found in all areas including Dongdo, Seodo, and Gajebawi Rock.

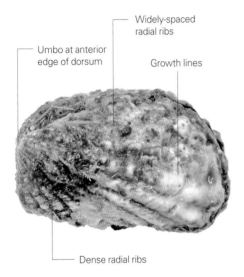

Umbo at anterior edge of dorsum

Widely-spaced radial ribs

Growth lines

Dense radial ribs

White gloss

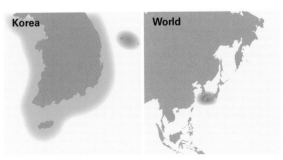

Korea

World

Solen gordonis Yokoyama, 1920

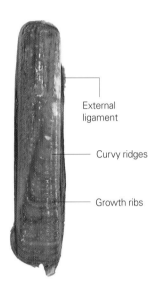

External
ligament

Curvy ridges

Growth ribs

Morphology

Shell large, slender, oblong, gaping at both ends. Umbo located anteriorly; ligament external. Surface smooth, shiny, covered with a greenish brown periostracum. Inside of shell reflecting external growth ribs. Ridges extending from umbo toward venter, weakly layered. Internal color mainly white; reddish along growth ribs at posterior margin. Pallial line thin, long. One tooth present under umbo. BL: about 110 mm long

Remarks

It is found in a sandy and muddy area in around 30 m deep subtidal zone. Shell deeply buried in the sand; the siphonal canal is stretched to the sand surface. It uses its siphonal canal to breath, and filter and eat organic matters. Solen species are all bamboo-shaped; particularly, Solen grandis and this species is most similar in shape. They differ in the location of umbo and the shell color, and especially the two types of sand they live in. *S. grandis* inhabits in a fine sandy area. The species that is commonly eaten is *S. strictus*, which mainly lives in the intertidal zone or shallow water.

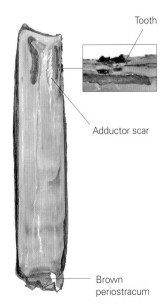

Tooth

Adductor scar

Brown
periostracum

Distribution

It is known as a large species ranging from Jeju Island in Korea to Boso Peninsula in Japan. It is distributed over the entire coast of Korea, and found mainly in the sandy area of the east coast of Dokdo.

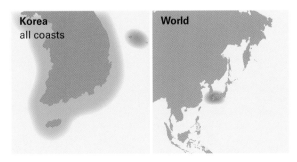

Korea
all coasts

World

Gari kazusensis (Yokoyama, 1922)

25 m depth

EN
RA
ES
IV
N

Morphology

Shell medium, elongate-oval, thin but solid, gaping posteriorly. Periostracum yellowish brown, peeled off at umbonal area. Umbo located anteriorly, ligament projected externally. Postero-dorsal margin straight. Ventral margin moderately round. Growth ribs clear, layered. Inside of shell white, with deeply-grooved pallial sinus. Two teeth and long ligamental ridge present. BL: about 50 mm long

Remarks

It is mainly found in coarse sandy areas mixed with mud in about 20 m deep (or deeper) subtidal zone. All 10 species are known in the Family Psammobiidae; most of them are purplish at the interior but this one is white. It has been observed mainly in the sandy areas of 25 m deep shores at the south of Dokdo wharf and 20-40 m deep coarse sandy shores at Namyang and Tongumi of Ulleungdo.

Distribution

It is a northern species occurring from the north-central part of Korea's East Sea to the northern Hokkaido in Japan. It is distributed in the northern East Sea, Ulleungdo and Dokdo in Korea. It was found on a sandy area at the south of Dongdo wharf in Dokdo.

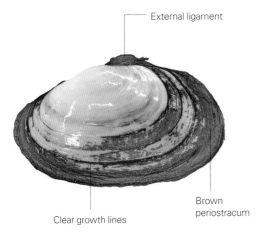

External ligament

Clear growth lines

Brown periostracum

2 teeth

Wide, long ligamental ridge

Round, deep pallial sinus

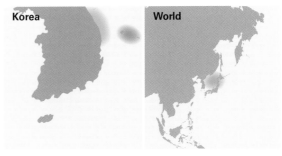

Korea

World

Irus irus (Linnaeus, 1758)

10 m depth

EN
RA
ES
IV
T

Morphology

Shell small, equivalve, almost rectangular, thick, solid. Umbo low, slanted anteriorly. Posterior margin long. Lamellae of growth ribs developed evenly; radial ribs densely arranged. Ventral margin with regularly-spaced lamellae; posterior margin with widely-spaced lamellae. Inside of shell white, with red margin. BL: about 15 mm long

Remarks

This species makes a hole to live in the lower intertidal zone to 20 m deep subtidal zone. In Korea, three species in genus *Irus* including *Irus mitis* and *Irus ishibashianus* are known to habitat in Korea. All three of them are similar in shape, and distinguished by the shape of lamellae, the space between growth ribs, and the shape and color of posterior margin. However, it is not easy to distinguish them as the variation frequently happens.

Distribution

It is distributed in Korea, Japan (below Honshu), China (coast of Yellow Sea-East China Sea), the Philippines, India, Thailand, Australia's northern and western coasts, the Red Sea, and the southeast coast of Africa. In Korea, it lives in Jeju Island, the southern West Sea (Gageodo), the South Sea, the southern East Sea, Ulleungdo and Dokdo. In Dokdo, it was observed from Gajebawi Rock.

Umbo

Lamellae of growth ribs

Narrower space between growth ribs at venter

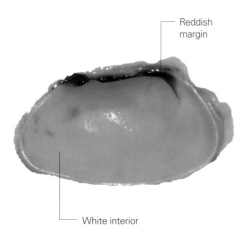

Reddish margin

White interior

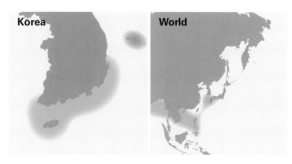

Korea

World

Paphia vernicosa (Gould, 1861)

25 m depth

EN
RA
ES
IV
T

Morphology

Shell elongate-oval. Color light brown. Valves thick, not inflated. Surface smooth, shiny, with 4 thick longitudinal bands. Growth ribs wrinkled, eroded, irregularly spaced, not deeply furrowed; specimen in Ulleungdo and Dokdo having 2-3 clear ribs. Inside of shell white, with a band extending downward from umbo, thick wrinkles reflecting interiorly. BL: about 75 mm long

Remarks

It lives in the sandy area of about 10-50 m deep subtidal zone. Some *Paphia* species live at a 200 m depth and have concentric growth ribs on the shell surface in common; 4 thick longitudinal bands from the umbo are their major feature. Each species is classified by the state of radial ribs and vertical bands, that is, their space, size and clarity. This species is named 'Red Venus Clam' in Korean, but 'Furrowed Venus Clam' was recorded as its first Korean name.

Distribution

It mainly occurs in Korea and Japan (southern Hokkaido-Kyushu), and shows the characteristics of temperate species. In Korea, it is distributed in Jeju Island, the southern West Sea (Gageodo), the South Sea, the southern East Sea, Ulleungdo and Dokdo. In Dokdo, it was observed on the sandy bottom of Dongdo.

Umbo tilted to anterior

4 radial bands

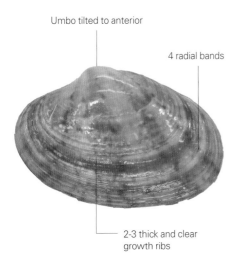

2-3 thick and clear growth ribs

Teeth

Brown band

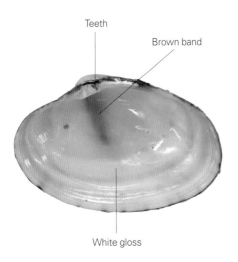

White gloss

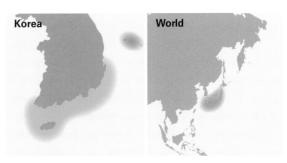

Korea

World

Corbula venusta Gould, 1861

25 m depth

EN
RA
ES
IV
T

Morphology

Shell small, swollen, brittle, broadly triangular at lower side. Left valve larger, covering right valve. Umbo centrally located. Postero-dorsal margin long. Ridges developed from umbo to posterior side. Periostracum yellowish brown. Inside of shell yellowish brown, with reddish margin. BL: about 7 mm long

Remarks

It is known to inhabit in the 10 m deep subtidal zone to 200 m depth. It lives mainly on the surface layer of sand, and because of its small size, it is not easily noticeable. When collecting samples, it is easy to find if the sand is stirred up.

Distribution

It is a temperate species occurring from Jeju Island in Korea to Japan (South Hokkaido to Kyushu). It is distributed on all coasts of Korea, and in Dokdo, it was observed in the sandy bottom of the south of Dongdo.

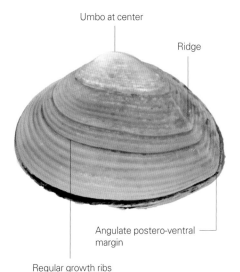

Umbo at center

Ridge

Angulate postero-ventral margin

Regular growth ribs

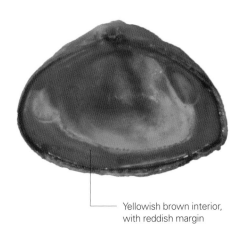

Yellowish brown interior, with reddish margin

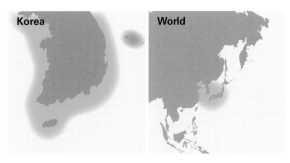

Korea

World

Hiatella arctica (Linnaeus, 1767)

Posterior end gaping

Reflected adductor scar

Ridges from umbo

Wrinkled growth line

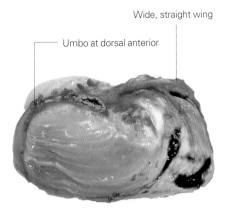

Wide, straight wing

Umbo at dorsal anterior

Morphology

Shell small, almost rectangular, varying in shape depending on substrate. Right valve larger, more swollen. Umbo located anteriorly. Postero-dorsal margin long ,with open end. Ventral margin straight. Ridge present from umbo to posterior side. Periostracum brown to yellowish-brown. Inside of shell yellowish-brown, glossy. Teeth absent. Pallial sinus shallowly depressed. BL: about 12 mm long

Remarks

It is usually found in shallow to 20 m deep (or deeper) waters and adheres to holdfasts of large brown algae such as *E. bicyclis* and *E. cava*. The shape variation is very high, and it is easily mistaken with the juveniles of *Entodesma navicula*, whose habitat is similar. The two species differ in the position of umbo and the shape of the postero-dorsal margin.

Distribution

It is a southern species occurring widely in Korea, Japan (Hokkaido-Kyushu) and Southeast Asia. It is distributed on all coasts of Korea, but no records have been found in the northern-central part of the West Sea. On Dokdo, it was observed in annexed islands in front of Dongdo and Seodo.

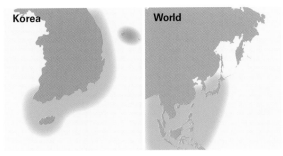

Korea

World

Entodesma navicula (Adams & Reeve, 1850)

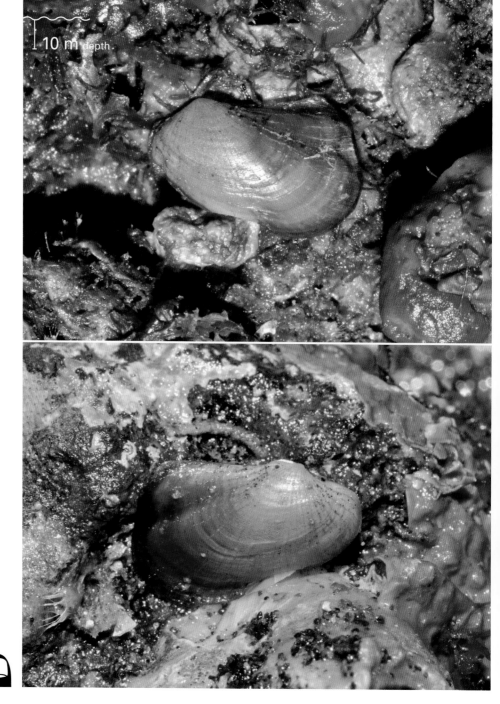

10 m depth

Morphology

Shell small, thin, brittle, swollen, highly variable in shape depending on substrates. Left valve larger, more swollen. Umbo tilted forward, with lined projections. Wing situated at posterior side of umbo; margin above wing straight. Ventral margin round. Juveniles commonly with black band along posterior margin. Inside of shell translucent, nacreous. BL: about 30 mm long

Remarks

It lives in substrates of large brown algae in the middle intertidal zone to 30 m deep subtidal zone. As it grows, the shell becomes darker from brown to walnut, and the torsion increases, making the right and left valves different. In Korea, four species are recorded in the Family Lyonsiidae, and before the torsion, a juvenile of this species is easily mistaken with *H. arctica*.

Distribution

It is a southern species occurring widely in Southeast Asia, including Korea and Japan (Hokkaido-Kyushu). In Korea, it is distributed in the central West Sea (Taean), in the South Sea, in the East Sea, on Ulleungdo and on Dokdo. On Dokdo, it was observed on the annexed islands in front of Dongdo and Seodo.

Straight margin

Round and tilted-forward umbo

Widely-spread wing

Fan-frame shaped radial ribs

Growth lines

Rounded postero-ventral margin

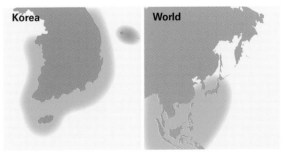

Korea

World

Class Cephalopoda

Cephalopoda has a characteristic in which the distinction of body parts becomes unclear as the head and feet develop. It includes squid, octopus, small octopus (*Octopus minor*), and pearly nautilus, and around 650 species are known worldwide. All are marine animals, and 22 species in 8 families are reported in Korea. It varies in size from 2–3 cm to several meters, and lives from shallow waters to depths of 1,000 m or deeper.

Cephalopod fossil records appear from the Cambrian. Shelled species are extremely rare, and usually with reduced shell or without shell. The mouth has a jaw plate looking like the beak, which holds the prey, and consumes it using the radula. The organ that sprays water is called a funnel, formed in the foot. Most cephalopods have pigment cells called chromatophore in their skin, enabling them to change the body color freely. Squids have three types of visual cells like humans, and octopus has one. All cephalopods except pearly nautilus have an ink sac.

Octopus vulgaris Cuvier, 1797

20 m depth

Morphology

Body muscular, head elliptical. Color usually reddish-brown, with yellow or blue spots. Surface of body covered with rough and pointed bumps horizontally. Width about 3/4 of the total length, sucker reddish brown. Large species growing over 1 m in length and weighs over 3 kg.

Remarks

It lives in the lower intertidal zone to the deep subtidal zone, and is nocturnal. The octopus (*Octopus dofleini*) is usually found on the east coast. It usually lives in deep water but rises to shallow water during spawning. *O. vulgaris* is observed in 5-30 m rocky waters of the east and south coasts all year round. The two species show differences in the protrusions on the body; *O. vulgaris* has them all over the body while *O. dofleini* usually has 3-4 protrusions on the upper part of the eye.

Distribution

This species is distributed from Jeju Island in Korea to south of Noto Peninsula in Japan. It is distributed on all coasts of Korea, but has not been reported in the central and northern West Sea. On Dokdo, it was observed in Dongdo, Seodo, Gajebawi Rock and annexed islands.

Eye

Yellow, purple spots

Irregular bumps

Reddish-brown suckers

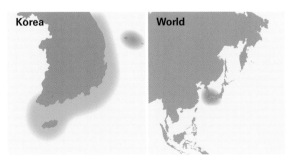

Korea

World

239

List of Dokdo's mollusks

We have put together the list of Phylum Mollusca of Dokdo and came up with a total of 173 species (4 classes, 5 subclasses, 20 orders, 72 families, 115 genera) including 10 newly confirmed species in 10 families which were found while taking photographs of other species. Kim (1978) made the first report on 7 molluscan species of Dokdo including 2 Polyplacophora and 5 Gastropoda, and afterwards, many more have been discovered through underwater surveys. The species found by year is as follows. Kim & Choe (1981) reported 18 species including 15 newly found species, Hong (1981) reported a total of 12 species with an addition of 4 species including *Crenomytilus grayanus*. Son & Hong (1992) reported 21 species with an addition of 11 species including *alliostoma haliarchus*. Choe & Lee (1994) reported 9 species with an addition of 8 Nudibranchia. Choe et al. (1996) reported 39 species with 13 unreported species. Je et al. (1998) recorded a total of 60 species through Dokdo Research Project with an addition of 31 species including *Ceraesignum maximum*. Dokdo Research and Preservation Association (DRPA) (1999) added 14 species recording a total of 48 species. The Dokdo & Ulleung Research Institute of Gyeongju University (DURI–GJU)(2004) recorded a total of 14 species with an addition of 3 species. Lee & Seo (2006) newly added 24 species recording a total of 68 species. Hwang et al. (2007) reported 45 species twice with an addition of 12 species in total (2 duplicates). National Institute of Fisheries Science (NFRDI) (2009) published a booklet on 57 species of mollusks with no newly added species. Ryu et al. (2012) reported a total of 45 species including 3 unreported species (1 duplicate). Kang et al. (2013) reported 14 species with no new addition.

The scientific names and classification system used in this book follow the system of World Register of Marine Species (WoRMS) (2014). The symbols displayed in species name are as follows: (a) refers to the 41 species whose scientific names have changed. (b) includes the 27 species whose habitats are not clear. They have been misidentified or not been found since their initial report. (c) refers to the species whose identification had been wrong. For example, Choe & Lee (1994) wrongly reported *Botobryon clavigerum Baba* as *N.wardi Odhner* which has been corrected in this list. (d) include the 8 species whose species names are difficult to confirm. They are reported as sp or *confer* without a specific epithet or impossible to confirm scientific name at all. (*) indicates that the species has been discovered for the first time through this research and was included in the text.

Phylum Mollusca 연체동물문

　Class Polyplacophora 다판강

　Subclass Neoloricata 신군부아강

　　Order Chitonida 군부목

　　Suborder Acanthochitonina 가시군부아목

　　　Family Acanthochitonidae 가시군부과

　　　　Genus *Acanthochitona* Gray, 1821 가시군부속

　　　　　[b]1. *Acanthochitona achates* (Gould, 1859) 좀털군부

　　　　　2. *Acanthochitona circellata* (A. Adams & Reeve MS, Reeve, 1847) 참털군부

　　　　　[b]3. *Acanthochitona defilippii* (Tapparone Canefri, 1874) 털군부

　　　Family Cryptoplacidae 털군부과

　　　　Genus *Cryptoplax* Blainville, 1818 털군부속

　　　　　4. *Cryptoplax japonica* Pilsbry, 1901 벌레군부

　　　Family Mopaliidae 따가리과

　　　　Genus *Placiphorella* Dall, 1879 따가리속

　　　　　5. *Placiphorella stimpsoni* (Gould, 1859) 따가리

　　　　Genus *Mopalia* Gray, 1847 수염군부속

　　　　　6. *Mopalia retifera* Thiele, 1909 수염군부

　　Suborder Chitonina 군부아목

　　　Family Chitonidae 군부과

　　　　Genus *Liolophura* Pilsbry, 1893

　　　　　7. *Liolophura japonica* (Lischke, 1873) 군부

　　　　Genus *Chiton* Linnaeus, 1758 군부속

　　　　　8. *Chiton* (*Rhyssoplax*) *kurodai* Is. & Iw. Taki, 1929 꼬마군부

　　　　　[b]9. *Chiton* (*Rhyssoplax*) *tectiformis* (Is. Taki, 1938)

　　　　Genus *Onithochiton* Gray, 1847 비단군부속

　　　　　10. *Onithochiton hirasei* Pilsbry, 1901 비단군부

　　　Family Ischnochitonidae 연두군부과

　　　　Genus *Ischnochiton* Gray, 1847 연두군부속

　　　　　[a]11. *Ischnochiton* (*Haploplax*) *comptus* (Gould, 1859) 연두군부

　　　　　[a]12. *Ischnochiton* (*Ischnochiton*) *boninensis* Bergenhayn, 193 가는줄연두군부

　　　　　[a,b]13. *Ischnochiton* (*Ischnochiton*) *hakodadensis* Carpenter in Pilsbry, 1893
　　　　　　　굵은줄연두군부

　　　　　[d]14. *Ischnochiton* sp.

　　　　Genus *Lepidozona* Pilsbry, 1892 줄군부속

　　　　　*15. *Lepidozona coreanica* (Reeve, 1874) 줄군부

　Class Gastropoda 복족강

　Subclass Patellogastropoda 삿갓조개아강

　　Family Lottiidae 두드럭배말과

　　　Genus *Lottia* Gray, 1833 두드럭배말속

　　　　16. *Lottia dorsuosa* (Gould, 1859) 두드럭배말

　　　　17. *Lottia langfordi* (Habe, 1944) 꼬마흰삿갓조개

　　　　18. *Lottia luchuana* (Pilsbry, 1901) 주름애기두드럭배말

　　　Genus *Patelloida* Quoy & Gaimard, 1834 배말속(신칭)

　　　　[b]19. *Patelloida heroldi* (Dunker, 1861) 애기두드럭배말

20. *Patelloida pygmaea* (Dunker, 1860) 애기배말
21. *Patelloida saccharina lanx* (Reeve, 1855) 테두리고둥

Genus *Nipponacmea* Sasaki & Okutani, 1993 배무래기속
  [a,b]22. *Nipponacmea fuscoviridis* (Teramachi, 1949) 납작배무래기
  [a]23. *Nipponacmea gloriosa* (Habe, 1944) 멋쟁이배무래기
  [a]24. *Nipponacmea schrenckii* (Lischke, 1868) 배무래기
  [a,b]25. *Nipponacmea nigrans* (Kira, 1961)

Genus *Niveotectura* Habe, 1944 흰삿갓조개속
  [a,*]26. *Niveotectura pallida* (Gould, 1859) 흰삿갓조개

Family Nacellidae 은배말과
  Genus *Cellana* H. Adams, 1869 진주배말속
    27. *Cellana grata* (Gould, 1859) 진주배말
    28. *Cellana nigrolineata* (Reeve, 1854) 흑색배말
    29. *Cellana toreuma* (Reeve, 1854) 애기삿갓조개

Subclass Vetigastropda 고복족아강
  Family Fissurellidae 구멍삿갓조개과
    Genus *Tugali* Gray, 1843 등줄삿갓조개속
      30. *Tugali decussata* A. Adams, 1852 흰이랑삿갓조개

    Genus *Macroschisma* Gray, 1835 긴구멍삿갓조개속
      31. *Macroschisma dilatatum* A. Adams, 1851 낮은구멍삿갓조개

  Family Haliotidae 전복과
    Genus *Haliotis* Linnaeus, 1758 전복속
      [a]32. *Haliotis discus* Reeve, 1846 둥근전복
      [a]33. *Haliotis gigantea* Gmelin, 1791 말전복
      [a]34. *Haliotis supertexta* Lischke, 1870 오분자기

  Family Colloniidae 팥알고둥과(신칭)
    Genus *Bothropoma* Thiele, 1924 쇄팥알고둥속(신칭)
      [a,b]35. *Bothropoma pilula* (Dunker, 1860) 쇄팥알고둥

    Genus *Homalopoma* Carpenter, 1864 팥알고둥속
      36. *Homalopoma amussitatum* (Gould, 1861) 누더기팥알고둥
      [b]37. *Homalopoma nocturnum* (Gould, 1861) 팥알고둥
      [b]38. *Homalopoma sangarense* (Schrenck, 1861) 산팥알고둥

  Family Phasianellidae 유리고둥과
    Genus *Tricolia* Risso, 1826 분홍유리고둥속(신칭)
      [a]39. *Tricolia variabilis* (Pease, 1861) 분홍유리고둥

  Family Chilodontidae Wenz, 1938 입술밤고둥과(신칭)
    Genus *Granata* Cotton, 1957
      *40. *Granata lyrata* (Pilsbry, 1890) 검은점갈비고둥

  Family Calliostomatidae 방석고둥과(신칭)
    Genus *Calliostoma* Swainson, 1840 방석고둥속
      [a,b]41. *Calliostoma haliarchus* (Melvill, 1889) 매끈이방석고둥
      [a]42. *Calliostoma multiliratum* (Sowerby II, 1875) 얼룩방석고둥
      [a,b]43. *Calliostoma simodense* Ikebe, 1942
      [a]44. *Calliostoma unicum* (Dunker, 1860) 방석고둥

  Family Stomatellidae 넓은입고둥과

Genus *Stomatolina* Iredale, 1937 넓은입고둥속
    *45. *Stomatolina rubra* (Lamarck, 1822) 넓은입고둥

Family Tegulidae 구멍밤고둥과(신칭)
  Genus *Chlorostoma* Swainson, 1840 밤고둥붙이속
    46. *Chlorostoma lischkei* (Tapparone-Canefri, 1874) 밤고둥
    47. *Chlorostoma turbinatum* (A. Adams, 1858) 구멍밤고둥
    [b]48. *Chlorostoma xanthostigma* (A. Adams, 1853) 명주고둥

  Genus *Tegula* Lesson, 1832
    [a]49. *Tegula pfeifferi* (Dunker, 1882) 팽이고둥

  Genus *Omphalius* Philippi, 1847 팽이고둥속
    50. *Omphalius nigerrimus* (Gmelin, 1791) 애기밤고둥
    51. *Omphalius rusticus* (Gmelin, 1791) 보말고둥

Family Trochidae 밤고둥과
  Genus *Cantharidus* Montfort, 1810 얼룩고둥속
    52. *Cantharidus bisbalteatus* Pilsbry, 1901 두줄얼룩고둥
    [b]53. *Cantharidus callichroa* (Philippi, 1849) 얼룩고둥
    54. *Cantharidus jessoensis* (Schrenck, 1863) 둥근입얼룩고둥
    *55. *Cantharidus japonicus* (A. Adams, 1853) 남방얼룩고둥

  Genus *Fossarina* A. Adams & Angas, 1864
    56. *Fossarina picta* A. Adams, 1864 흰구름무늬꼬마고둥

  Genus *Diloma* Philippi, 1845
    57. *Diloma piperina* (Philippi, 1849) 띠각시고둥

  Genus *Monodonta* Lamarck, 1799 울타리고둥속
    [a,b]58. *Monodonta confusa* Tapparone Canefri, 1874 개울타리고둥
    59. *Monodonta neritoides* (Philippi, 1849) 각시고둥
    60. *Monodonta perplexa* Pilsbry, 1889 깜장각시고둥

Family Turbinidae 소라과
  Genus *Turbo* Linnaeus, 1758 소라속
    61. *Turbo cornutus* Lightfoot, 1786 소라
    [d]62. *Turbo* cf. *excellens* G. B. Sowerby III, 1914
    [b]63. *Turbo stenogyrus* P. Fischer, 1873 민소라

  Genus *Pomaulax* Gray, 1850 납작소라속
    64. *Pomaulax japonicus* (Dunker, 1845) 납작소라

Subclass Caenogastropoda 신생복족아강
  Order [unassigned] Caenogastropoda 신생복족목
    Family Potamididae 갯고둥과
      Genus *Cerithidea* Swainson, 1840 비틀이고둥속
        [a]65. *Cerithidea balteata* A. Adams, 1855 얼룩비틀이고둥

    Family Litiopidae 홀쭉이고둥과
      Genus *Styliferina* A. Adams, 1860
        66. *Styliferina goniochila* A. Adams, 1860 흰반점홀쭉이고둥

    Family Triphoridae 띠줄고둥과
      Genus *Iniforis* Jousseaume, 1884
        [d]67. *Iniforis* sp.

Genus *Mastonia* Hinds, 1843

ᵈ68. *Mastonia* sp.

Order Littorinimorpha

　Family Calyptraeidae 배고둥과

　　Genus *Crepidula* Lamarck, 1799 뚱뚱이짚신고둥속

　　　69. *Crepidula onyx* G. B. Sowerby I, 1824 뚱뚱이짚신고둥

　　Genus *Bostrycapulus* Olsson & Harbison, 1953 침배고둥속

　　　70. *Bostrycapulus gravispinosus* (Kuroda & Habe, 1950) 침배고둥

　Family Capulidae 매부리고둥과

　　Genus *Capulus* Montfort, 1810 매부리고둥속

　　　71. *Capulus danieli* (Crosse, 1858) 매부리고둥

　Family Cypraeidae 개오지과

　　Genus *Purpuradusta* Schilder, 1939 점박이개오지속

　　　72. *Purpuradusta gracilis* (Gaskoin, 1849) 점박이개오지

　Family Ovulidae 개오지붙이과

　　Genus *Sandalia* Cate, 1973 주홍토끼고둥속(신칭)

　　　ᵃ73. *Sandalia triticea* (Lamarck, 1810) 주홍토끼고둥

　Family Littorinidae 총알고둥과

　　Genus *Littorina* Férussac, 1822 총알고둥속

　　　74. *Littorina brevicula* (Philippi, 1844) 총알고둥

　　　ᵇ75. *Littorina mandshurica* (Schrenk, 1861)

　　Genus *Echinolittorina* Habe, 1956 좁쌀무늬총알고둥속

　　　ᵃ76. *Echinolittorina radiata* (Souleyet in Eydoux & Souleyet, 1852) 좁쌀무늬총알고둥

　Family Ranellidae 수염고둥과

　　Genus *Monoplex* Perry, 1810 각시수염고둥속

　　　ᵃ˙*77. *Monoplex parthenopeus* (Salis Marschlins, 1793) 각시수염고둥

　Family Hipponicidae 고깔고둥과

　　Genus *Hipponix* Defrance, 1819 기생고깔고둥속

　　　78. *Hipponix conicus* (Schumacher, 1817) 기생고깔고둥

　Family Velutinidae 배고둥붙이과

　　Genus *Lamellaria* Montagu, 1815 긴입배고둥붙이속(신칭)

　　　79. *Lamellaria kiiensis* Habe, 1944 긴입배고둥붙이

　Family Vermetidae 뱀고둥과

　　Genus *Ceraesignum* Golding, Bieler, Rawlings & Collins, 2014 뱀고둥속(신칭)

　　　ᵃ˙ᵇ80. *Ceraesignum maximum* (G.B. Sowerby I, 1825) 뱀고둥

　　Genus *Thylacodes* Guettard, 1770 큰뱀고둥속

　　　ᵃ81. *Thylacodes adamsii* (Mörch, 1859) 큰뱀고둥

Order Neogastropoda 신복족목

　Family Buccinidae 물레고둥과

　　Genus *Cantharus* Röding, 1798 털껍질돼지고둥속

　　　ᵇ82. *Cantharus cecillei* Philippi, 1844 털껍질돼지고둥

　　Genus *Engina* Gray, 1839 구슬띠물레고둥속

　　　83. *Engina menkeana* (Dunker, 1860) 구슬띠물레고둥

Genus *Kelletia* Bayle in P. Fischer, 1884 매끈이고둥속
    84. *Kelletia lischkei* Kuroda, 1938 매끈이고둥

Genus *Pollia* Gray, 1834 쇠털껍질고둥속
    85. *Pollia subrubiginosa* (E. A. Smith, 1879) 쇠털껍질고둥

Family Columbellidae 무륵과
  Genus *Anachis* H. Adams & A. Adams, 1853 보살무륵속
    86. *Anachis miser* (G. B. Sowerby I, 1844) 보살고둥

  Genus *Mitrella* Risso, 1826 보리무륵속
    87. *Mitrella bicincta* (Gould, 1860) 보리무륵

Family Nassariidae 좁쌀무늬고둥과
  Genus *Nassarius* Duméril, 1805 좁쌀무늬고둥속
    88. *Nassarius fraterculus* (Dunker, 1860) 검은줄좁쌀무늬고둥
    ᵈ89. *Nassarius* cf. *glans glans* (Linnaeus, 1758)

Family Muricidae 뿔소라과
  Genus *Ergalatax* Iredale, 1931 탑뿔고둥속
    90. *Ergalatax contracta* (Reeve, 1846) 탑뿔고둥

  Genus *Ceratostoma* Herrmannsen, 1846 맵사리속
    91. *Ceratostoma rorifluum* (Adams & Reeve, 1849) 맵사리

  Genus *Reishia* Kuroda & Habe, 1971 대수리속
    92. *Reishia bronni* (Dunker, 1860) 두드럭고둥
    93. *Reishia clavigera* (Küster, 1860) 대수리
    94. *Reishia luteostoma* (Holten, 1803) 뿔두드럭고둥

Subclass Heterobranchia 이새아강
Infraclass [unassigned] Heterobranchia 이새하강
  Family Siphonariidae 고랑딱개비과
    Genus *Siphonaria* G. B. Sowerby I, 1823 고랑딱개비속
      95. *Siphonaria sirius* Pilsbry, 1894 꽃고랑딱개비
      96. *Siphonaria japonica* (Donovan, 1824) 고랑딱개비

Infraclass Opisthobranchia 후새하강
  Order Cephalaspidea 두순목
    Family Haminoeidae 포도고둥과
      Genus *Haminoea* Turton & Kingston in Carrington, 1830 포도고둥속
        ᵃ97. *Haminoea japonica* Pilsbry, 1895 포도고둥

  Order Sacoglossa 낭설목
    Family Limapontiidae 꼭지갯민숭붙이과
      Genus *Placida* Trinchese, 1876
        98. *Placida cremoniana* (Trinchese, 1892) 검정돌기갯민숭붙이

    Family Plakobranchidae 날씬이갯민숭붙이과
      Genus *Elysia* Risso, 1818 날씬이갯민숭붙이속
        ᵃ99. *Elysia atroviridis* Baba, 1955 초록날씬이갯민숭붙이
        100. *Elysia abei* Baba, 1955 녹색날씬이갯민숭붙이

  Order Anaspidea 무순목
    Family Aplysiidae 군소과
      Genus *Aplysia* Linnaeus, 1767 군소속

101. *Aplysia kurodai* Baba, 1937 군소

102. *Aplysia juliana* Quoy & Gaimard, 1832 말군소

103. *Aplysia oculifera* A. Adams & Reeve, 1850 안경무늬군소

104. *Aplysia parvula* Mörch, 1863 검은테군소

105. *Aplysia sagamiana* Baba, 1949 갈색군소

Order Pleurobranchomorpha 군소붙이목

Family Pleurobranchaeidae 군소붙이과

Genus *Pleurobranchaea* Leue, 1813 올빼미군소붙이속

106. *Pleurobranchaea japonica* Thiele, 1925 올빼미군소붙이

Genus *Berthellina* Gardiner, 1936 빨강갯민달팽이속

107. *Berthellina citrina* (Rüppell & Leuckart, 1828) 빨강갯민달팽이

Order Nudibranchia 나새목

Family Facelinidae 하늘소갯민숭이과

Genus *Hermissenda* Bergh, 1879 하늘소갯민숭이속

108. *Hermissenda crassicornis* (Eschscholtz, 1831) 하늘소갯민숭이

Genus *Sakuraeolis* Baba, 1965 눈송이갯민숭이속

109. *Sakuraeolis japonica* (Baba, 1937) 눈송이갯민숭이

Family Pleurolidiidae 검정갯민숭이과(신칭)

Genus *Protaeolidiella* Baba, 1955 검정갯민숭이속

110. *Protaeolidiella atra* Baba, 1955 검정갯민숭이

Family Fionidae 주름도롱이갯민숭이과

Genus *Fiona* Alder & Hancock [in Forbes & Hanley], 1853 주름도롱이갯민숭이속

[b]111. *Fiona pinnata* (Eschscholtz, 1831) 주름도롱이갯민숭이

Family Scyllaeidae 사슴갯민숭이과

Genus *Notobryon* Odhner, 1936 사슴갯민숭이속

112. *Notobryon clavigerum* Baba, 1937 사슴갯민숭이

Family Tritoniidae 예쁜이갯민숭이과

Genus *Tritonia* Cuvier, 1798 예쁜이갯민숭이속

113. *Tritonia festiva* (Stearns, 1873) 예쁜이갯민숭이

Family Arminidae 줄무늬갯민숭이과

Genus *Dermatobranchus* van Hasselt, 1824 등줄무늬갯민숭이속(신칭)

114. *Dermatobranchus otome* Baba, 1992 아가씨줄무늬갯민숭이

Family Cadlinidae 노란갯민숭달팽이과

Genus *Cadlina* Bergh, 1878 노란테갯민숭달팽이속

115. *Cadlina japonica* Baba, 1937 노란테갯민숭달팽이

Genus *Aldisa* Bergh, 1878 점박이붉은갯민숭달팽이속

116. *Aldisa cooperi* Robilliard & Baba, 1972 점박이붉은갯민숭달팽이

Family Chromodorididae 갯민숭달팽이과

Genus *Chromodoris* Alder & Hancock, 1855 갯민숭달팽이속

117. *Chromodoris orientalis* Rudman, 1983 흰갯민숭달팽이

Genus *Goniobranchus* Pease, 1866

[a]118. *Goniobranchus tinctorius* (Rüppell & Leuckart, 1830) 망사갯민숭달팽이

[a]119. *Goniobranchus aureopurpureus* (Collingwood, 1881) 점점갯민숭달팽이

Genus *Hypselodoris* Stimpson, 1855 파랑갯민숭달팽이속
   120. *Hypselodoris festiva* (A. Adams, 1861) 파랑갯민숭달팽이

Family Discodorididae 낮은갯민숭달팽이과(신칭)
   Genus *Platydoris* Bergh, 1877 구름갯민숭달팽이속
     [a]121. *Platydoris ellioti* (Alder & Hancock, 1864) 구름갯민숭달팽이

Family Dorididae 갑옷갯민숭달팽이과
   Genus *Homoiodoris* Bergh, 1882 두드럭갯민숭달팽이속
     122. *Homoiodoris japonica* Bergh, 1882 두드럭갯민숭달팽이

Family Goniodorididae 불꽃갯민숭이과
   Genus *Okenia* Menke, 1830 불꽃갯민숭이속
     [a]123. *Okenia hiroi* (Baba, 1938) 불꽃갯민숭이

Family Dendrodorididae 수지갯민숭달팽이과
   Genus *Dendrodoris* Ehrenberg, 1831 수지갯민숭달팽이속
     [a]124. *Dendrodoris krusensternii* (Gray, 1850) 여왕갯민숭달팽이

Class Bivalvia 이매패강
Order Mytiloida 홍합목
   Family Mytilidae 홍합과
     Genus *Brachidontes* Swainson, 1840
       [a]125. *Brachidontes mutabilis* (Gould, 1861) 주름담치

     Genus *Crenomytilus* Soot-Ryen, 1955
       [b]126. *Crenomytilus grayanus* (Dunker, 1853) 동해담치

     Genus *Leiosolenus* Carpenter, 1857
       [a]127. *Leiosolenus lischkei* Huber, 2010 애기돌맛조개

     Genus *Modiolus* Lamarck, 1799
       [b]128. *Modiolus auriculatus* (Krauss, 1848) 깃털담치
       129. *Modiolus modiolus* (Linnaeus, 1758) 털담치
       130. *Modiolus nipponicus* (Oyama, 1950) 개적구
       [b]131. *Modiolus philippinarum* (Hanley, 1843)

     Genus *Mytilus* Linnaeus, 1758
       132. *Mytilus coruscus* Gould, 1861 홍합
       [b]133. *Mytilus galloprovincialis* Lamarck, 1819 지중해담치

     Genus *Septifer* Dunker, 1848
       134. *Septifer bilocularis* (Linnaeus, 1758) 두눈격판담치
       135. *Septifer keenae* Nomura, 1936 격판담치
       136. *Septifer virgatus* (Wiegmann, 1837) 굵은줄격판담치

Order Arcoida 돌조개목
   Family Arcidae 돌조개과
     Genus *Arca* Linnaeus, 1758
       137. *Arca boucardi* Jousseaume, 1894 긴네모돌조개
       [a,b]138. *Arca patriarchalis* Röding, 1798 돌조개

   Family Parallelodontidae 왕복털조개과
     Genus *Porterius* Clark, 1925
       139. *Porterius dalli* (E. A. Smith, 1885) 왕복털조개

Order Limoida 외투조개목

Family Limidae 외투조개과
　Genus *Limaria* Link, 1807
　　140. *Limaria hirasei* (Pilsbry, 1901) 얇은납작개가리비

Order Ostreoida 굴목
　Family Gryphaeidae 주름굴과
　　Genus *Neopycnodonte* Stenzel, 1971
　　　141. *Neopycnodonte cochlear* (Poli, 1795) 주름꼬마굴

　Family Ostreidae 굴과
　　Genus *Crassostrea* Sacco, 1897
　　　142. *Crassostrea gigas* (Thunberg, 1793) 굴
　　　143. *Crassostrea nippona* (Seki, 1934) 바위굴

　　Genus *Saccostrea* Dollfus & Dautzenberg, 1920
　　　ᵇ144. *Saccostrea echinata* (Quoy & Gaimard, 1835) 가시굴

　　Genus *Striostrea* Vialov, 1936
　　　145. *Striostrea circumpicta* (Pilsbry, 1904) 태생굴

　　Genus *Ostrea* Linnaeus, 1758 굴속
　　　ᵈ146. *Ostrea* sp.

Order Pectinoida 가리비목
　Family Anomiidae 잠쟁이과
　　Genus *Anomia* Linnaeus, 1758
　　　147. *Anomia chinensis* Philippi, 1849 개굴잠쟁이

　Family Pectinidae 가리비과
　　Genus *Laevichlamys* Waller, 1993
　　　ᵃ148. *Laevichlamys cuneata* (Reeve, 1853) 짝귀비단가리비

　Family Spondylidae 국화조개과
　　Genus *Spondylus* Linnaeus, 1758
　　　ᵇ149. *Spondylus butleri* Reeve, 1856 가시국화조개
　　　ᵃ.*150. *Spondylus squamosus* Schreibers, 1793 국화조개
　　　151. *Spondylus varius* G. B. Sowerby I, 1827 접시국화조개

Order Veneroida 백합목
　Family Chamidae 굴아재비과
　　Genus *Amphichama* Habe, 1964
　　　152. *Amphichama argentata* (Kuroda & Habe, 1958)

　　Genus *Chama* Linnaeus, 1758
　　　153. *Chama dunkeri* Lischke, 1870 맨드라미굴아재비
　　　154. *Chama fragum* Reeve, 1847 굴아재비
　　　155. *Chama japonica* Lamarck, 1819 햇빛굴아재비
　　　156. *Chama limbula* Lamarck, 1819 보라굴아재비

　　Genus *Pseudochama* Odhner, 1917
　　　157. *Pseudochama retroversa* (Lischke, 1870) 보라왼돌이굴아재비

　Family Kelliidae 큰집가재더부사리조개과
　　Genus *Kellia* Turton, 1822 큰집가재더부사리조개속
　　　ᵈ158. *Kellia lischkei* (sic.)
　　　159. *Kellia porculus* Pilsbry, 1904 아기가재더부사리조개

Family Lasaeidae 가재더부사리조개과
Genus *Lasaea* Brown, 1827
160. *Lasaea undulata* (Gould, 1861) 파도가재더부사리조개

Family Psammobiidae 자패과
Genus *Gari* Schumacher, 1817 나무껍질빛조개속(신칭)
ᵃ.*161. *Gari kazusensis* (Yokoyama, 1922) 나무껍질빛조개

Family Tellinidae 접시조개과
Genus *Macoma* Leach, 1819 대양조개속(신칭)
162. *Macoma incongrua* (Martens, 1865) 애기대양조개

Family Veneridae 백합과
Genus *Irus* F. C. Schmidt, 1818 주름입조개속(신칭)
163. *Irus irus* (Linnaeus, 1758) 굵은주름입조개
164. *Irus mitis* (Deshayes, 1854) 주름입조개

Genus *Paphia* Röding, 1798
*165. *Paphia vernicosa* (Gould, 1861) 밭고랑행달조개(붉은행달조개)

Order Carditoida 주름방사늑조개목
Family Carditidae 주름방사늑조개과
Genus *Cardita* Bruguière, 1792
166. *Cardita leana* Dunker, 1860 주름방사늑조개

Order [unassigned] Euheterodonta
Family Gastrochaenidae 구멍뚫이조개과
Genus *Gastrochaena* Spengler, 1783 구멍뚫이조개속
ᵈ167. *Gastrochaena* sp. 구멍뚫이조개류

Family Hiatellidae 족사부착쇄조개과
Genus *Hiatella* Bosc, 1801 족사부착쇄조개속
ᵃ168. *Hiatella arctica* (Linnaeus, 1767) 족사부착쇄조개

Family Solenidae 죽합과
Genus *Solen* Linnaeus, 1758 죽합속
*169. *Solen gordonis* Yokoyama, 1920 붉은맛

Order Anomalodesmata 이인대목
Family Lyonsiidae 안쪽인대조개과
Genus *Entodesma* Philippi, 1845 안쪽인대조개속
170. *Entodesma navicula* (Adams & Reeve, 1850) 안쪽인대조개

Order Myoida 우럭목
Family Corbulidae 쇄방사늑조개과
Genus *Corbula* Bruguière, 1797 쇄방사늑조개속
ᵃ.*171. *Corbula venusta* Gould, 1861 예쁜이쇄방사늑조개

Class Cephalopoda 두족강
Order Octopoda 문어목
Family Octopodidae 문어과
Genus *Enteroctopus* Rochebrune & Mabille, 1889
ᵃ172. *Enteroctopus dofleini* (Wülker, 1910) 문어

Genus *Octopus* Cuvier, 1798 문어속
173. *Octopus vulgaris* Cuvier, 1797 왜문어

Literature

Choe BL, 1992.
Illustrated encyclopedia of fauna and flora of Korea. Vol. 33, Mollusca (II). Ministry of Education, Seoul, pp. 1-860 (in Korean).

Choe BL, Lee JR, 1994.
Opisthobranchs (Mollusca: Gastopoda) from Ullung and Dong-do Islands, Korea. Korean Journal of Zoology, 37:352-376.

Choe BL, Park JK, Lee JR, 1996.
Marine molluscs of Ulrung and Tokdo Islands. *In*: Report on the Survey of Natural Environment in Korea. The Ulleung and Dokdo Islands. Korean National Council for the Conservation of Nature, 10:353-411 (in Korean).

DRPA, 1999.
Fundamental study on environment and conservation of fishery resources in Dokdo and its adjacent coast. Dokdo Research Series 4. Dokdo Research and Preservation Association (DRPA), Seoul, pp. 1-253 (in Korean).

DURI-GJU, 2004.
Survey on the wildness area, Dokdo Island. Ulleung-gun, Korea. Dokdo and Ulleung Research Institute of Gyungju Univ. (DURI-GJU), pp. 1-450 (in Korean).

EOL, 2014.
Encyclopedia of Life, Available from http://www.eol.org. Accessed 2014-10-27.

Habe T, 1977.
Systematics of Mollusca in Japan. Bivalvia and Scaphopoda. Hokuryukan, Tokyo, pp. 1-372 (in Japanese).

Hong JS, 1981.
SCUBA observations of marine benthos in Dokdo. *In*: A report on the scientific survey of the Ulreung and Dogdo islands. The Report of KACN, 19:229-236 (in Korean).

Hwang UW, Ryu SH, Jang KH, Choi EH, Kim SK, Bahn SY, 2007.
Marine invertebrates of Dogdo. In: Monitoring report on natural mounument 336, Dokdo island natural reserve. Cultural Heritage Administration, Seoul, pp. 1-28 (in Korean).

Je JG, Lee SW, Shin SH, Ko CH, 1998.
Zoogeographical distribution of molluscs on rocky bottom of Dokdo: *In* Fundamental study on environment and conservation of fishery resources in Dokdo and its adjacent coast, eds. Dokdo Research Series 4. Seoul: Dokdo Research and Preservation Association, pp. 1-253 (in Korean)

Kang DW, Seo SY, Kang JS, Paek WK, 2013.
Diversity of intertidal benthic invertebrate of Dokdo and Ullenung-do island from Korea. Journal of Asia-Pacific Biodiversity 6(1):157-164.

Kim HS, 1978.
Report on the collection of coastal marine invertebrates of Dokdo. Cons. Nat. Nat. Res., 23:13–15 (in Korean)

Kim HS, Choe BL, 1981.
The fauna of marine invertebrate in Ulreung Is. and Dogdo Is. *In*: A report on the scientific survey of the Ulreung and Dogdo islands. The Report of KACN, 19:193–200 (in Korean).

Lee JR, Seo SJ, 2006.
Marine invertebrates I (Porifera, Mollusca and Annelida) of Dokdo. Ministry of the Environment, Seoul, pp. 1–28 (in Korean).

Min DK, 2004.
Mollusks in Korea. Hangul Graphics, Seoul, pp. 1–566 (in Korea).

Ministry of Environment (Daegu Office), 2007.
Detailed investigation report on ecosystem in Dokdo

NFRDI, 2009.
Marine fauna and flora in Dokdo. Korea. National Fisheries Research and Development Institute (NFRDI), pp. 1–225 (in Korean).

Okutani T, 2000.
Marine mollusks in Japan. Tokai University Press, Tokyo, pp. 1–1173.

Rudman WB, 2000.
Sea Slug Forum. Australian Museum, Sydney. Available from http://www.seaslugforum.net. Accessed 2014-10-27.

Ryu SH, Jang KH, Choi EH, Kim SK, Song SJ, Cho HJ, Ryu JS, Kim YM, Sagong J, Lee JH, Yeo MY, Bahn SY, Kim HM, Lee GS, Lee DH, Choo YS, Park JH, Park JS, Ryu JS, Khim JS, Hwang UW, 2012. Biodiversity of marine invertebrates on rocky shores of Dokdo, Korea. Zoological Studies 51(5):710–726.

Son MH, Hong SY, 1992.
A catalogue of marine molluscs of Dogdo Island. Island Res. Soc. of Korea, 1 (Dokdo Island Expedition Special Report):71–88 (in Korea).

WoRMS Editorial Board, 2014.
World Register of Marine Species. Available from http://www.marinespecies.org at VLIZ. Accessed 2014-10-27.

Scientific names

A

Acanthochitona circellata 42

Aldisa cooperi 164

Anomia chinensis 214

Aplysia juliana 140

Aplysia kurodai 138

Aplysia parvula 142

Arca boucardi 184

B

Berthellina delicata 146

C

Cadlina japonica 152

Calliostoma multiliratum 74

Calliostoma unicum 76

Cantharidus bisbalteatus 64

Cantharidus japonicus 68

Cantharidus jessoensis 66

Cardita leana 220

Cellana grata 86

Cellana toreuma 88

Ceratostoma rorifluum 118

Chama japonica 216

Chiton (Rhyssoplax) kurodai 36

Chlorostoma lischkei 56

Chlorostoma turbinatum 58

Chromodoris orientalis 156

Corbula venusta 230

Crassostrea gigas 210

Crassostrea nippona 212

Crepidula onyx 96

Cryptoplax japonica 44

D

Dendrodoris krusensternii 166

Dermatobranchus otome 168

E

Echinolittorina radiata 102

Elysia abei 136

Elysia atroviridis 134

Engina menkeana 126

Entodesma navicula 234

Ergalatax contracta 120

G

Gari kazusensis 224

Goniobranchus aureopurpureus 160

Goniobranchus tinctorius 158

Gorbula venusta 230

Granata lyrate 80

H

Haliotis discus 48

Haliotis supertexta 50

Haminoea japonica 132

Hermissenda crassicornis 172

Hiatella arctica 232

Hipponix conicus 104

Homalopoma amussitatum 78

Homoiodoris japonica 154

Hypselodoris festiva 162

I

Irus irus 226

Ischnochiton (Haploplax) comptus 26

Ischnochiton (Ischnochiton)
   boninensis 28

K

Kelletia lischkei 128

Kellia porculus 218

L

Laevichlamys cuneata 200
Leiosolenus lischkei 190
Lepidozona coreanica 30
Limaria hirasei 204
Liolophura japonica 38
Littorina brevicula 100
Lottia dorsuosa 90

M

Macroschisma dilatatum 54
Mitrella bicincta 122
Modiolus modiolus 192
Modiolus nipponicus 194
Monodonta perplexa 70
Monoplex parthenopeus 110
Mopalia retifera 34
Mytilus coruscus 188

N

Nassarius fraterculus 124
Neopycnodonte cochlear 206
Nipponacmea schrenckii 92
Niveotectura pallida 94

O

Octopus vulgaris 238
Okenia hiroi 148
Omphalius rusticus 62
Onithochiton hirasei 40

P

Paphia vernicosa 228
Placiphorella stimpsoni 32
Platydoris ellioti 150
Pleurobranchaea japonica 144
Pollia subrubiginosa 130
Pomaulax japonicus 84
Porterius dalli 186
Protaeolidiella atra 176
Purpuradusta gracilis 98

R

Reishia bronni 112
Reishia clavigera 114
Reishia luteostoma 116

S

Sakuraeolis japonica 174
Sandalia triticea 106
Septifer keenae 196
Septifer virgatus 198
Siphonaria japonica 180
Siphonaria sirius 178
Solen gordonis 222
Spondylus squamosus 202
Stomatolina rubra 72
Striostrea circumpicta 208

T

Tegula pfeifferi 60
Thylacodes adamsii 108
Tritonia festiva 170
Tugali decussata 52
Turbo cornutus 82